29.95

St. Patrick
of Ireland

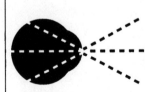

This Large Print Book carries the
Seal of Approval of N.A.V.H.

St. Patrick of Ireland

A Biography

Philip Freeman

Thorndike Press • Waterville, Maine

**Library of Congress Control Number: 2004103188
ISBN 0-7862-6594-9 (lg. print : hc : alk. paper)**

St. Patrick
of Ireland

As the Founder/CEO of NAVH, the only national health agency solely devoted to those who, although not totally blind, have an eye disease which could lead to serious visual impairment, I am pleased to recognize Thorndike Press* as one of the leading publishers in the large print field.

Founded in 1954 in San Francisco to prepare large print textbooks for partially seeing children, NAVH became the pioneer and standard setting agency in the preparation of large type.

Today, those publishers who meet our standards carry the prestigious "Seal of Approval" indicating high quality large print. We are delighted that Thorndike Press is one of the publishers whose titles meet these standards. We are also pleased to recognize the significant contribution Thorndike Press is making in this important and growing field.

Lorraine H. Marchi, L.H.D.
Founder/CEO
NAVH

* Thorndike Press encompasses the following imprints: Thorndike, Wheeler, Walker and Large Print Press.

Acknowledgments

I am deeply grateful to the many people who directly and indirectly contributed to this book. I gave many a gray hair to my professors over the years as they worked patiently to instruct me in Greek and Latin, thus my special thanks to Gregory Nagy, Thomas Palaima, and Cynthia Shelmerdine. My teachers at the Department of Celtic Languages and Literatures at Harvard University, especially Patrick Ford, John Koch, and John Carey, first introduced me to the fascinating world of early Ireland. However, I owe the most gratitude to my students, who have always challenged me to look at history and literature through new eyes.

Many thanks also to St. Patrick's Cathedral in Armagh; Trinity College, Dublin; the National Museum of Wales; and the National Museum of Ireland for allowing me to publish objects from their collections, and to Sean Tomkins for his beautiful photographs. Joëlle Delbourgo believed in the book from the beginning and made it happen, as did Robert Bender and Johanna Li. As always, nothing would have been possible without the support of my wife, Alison.

Contents

Preface

The world ended in A.D. 410 — on August 24 to be precise. That was the day Alaric and his band of Germanic Visigoths entered the city of Rome, sacking and looting the capital of the greatest empire the world had ever known. For over five hundred years, Rome had ruled the world from Spain to Syria and north to the land of the Celts. The fall of the city sent a shudder through the Mediterranean lands, but in Roman Britain no one even noticed. Britain had been Roman since the emperor Claudius crossed the channel with his legions in A.D. 43, but years of raids by hostile neighbors and neglect from the imperial government left the land with little time to mourn distant Rome. Saxons, Picts, and Irish sporadically ransacked the countryside, homegrown tyrants were rising throughout the island, and the Christian church of Britain was being torn apart by dangerous heresies.

The collapse of the Roman power was, however, welcome news to the Irish who made their living raiding isolated British farms for slaves. Women were best, as they could serve their masters both in the fields and in their beds. Grown men were difficult to handle and were often killed, but young boys could be broken more easily and were useful in the dirty and dull tasks of farm life. The withdrawal of the Roman navy from the Irish Sea made more daring raids possible, so one moonless night in late summer we can imagine that a few boats slipped into the narrow waterway separating Ireland from Britain and headed for a tempting prize — the rich settlements on Britain's western coast, a land that included scores of poorly protected villas.

As the boats neared the shore, the sails were lowered from a single mast. Each of the raiders manned a sturdy oak oar to maneuver the hide-covered boats. Quickly and silently they slipped over the side into the water and carefully pulled their leather and wood-framed vessels onto the beach. A few men were left behind to guard the boats — no fires, no laughing, no talking above a whisper. If the boats were discovered and the alarm sounded, the raiders had no hope of seeing their island home again.

Their footsteps were muffled as the men

marched inland through the fields, avoiding the roads patrolled sporadically by a volunteer local militia. At last in the distance they could see their destination — a collection of buildings behind a low stone wall. This was the modest but prosperous villa of a local nobleman, a small two-story building with no more than a dozen rooms facing a courtyard next to a few barns used for housing livestock, grain, and slaves. The wall surrounding the structures stood no higher than a man's neck and served more to keep poultry from wandering than to repel invaders.

The Irishmen quickly moved over the wall or perhaps through an unlocked gate, with most slipping into the servants' quarters while a handful carefully worked up the stairs of the main building into the sleeping chambers of the owners.

The young man in the second bedroom had no time to fight back. His parents were away in the nearby fortified town of Bannaventa Berniae, where his father served on the city council. He was alone on the villa's second floor with only a few household servants downstairs when the raiders entered his room. They had him gagged and bound before he was fully awake. A chain was fastened around his neck, and along with the villa's servants he was marched off in line to the waiting boat. Surely someone from the local guard would rescue him. Surely his parents would pay anything to ransom him. But the raiders moved with a swift efficiency, killing any captives who cried out for help or slowed them down. And there was no hope of rescue — the wild island where he was heading was beyond the reach of civilized Britain. His life of privilege and luxury was over — Patricius, known to later ages as Saint Patrick, was now a slave.

THE CELTIC LANDS

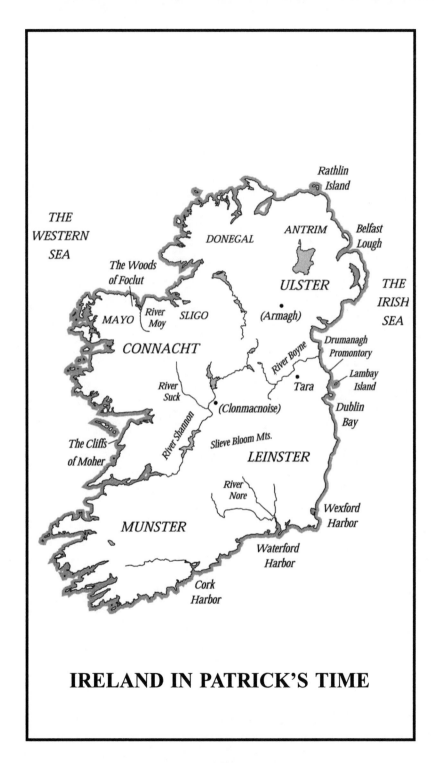

IRELAND IN PATRICK'S TIME

Introduction

Patrick's Life and Letters

Fifteen centuries ago an old man in Ireland wrote two of the most remarkable letters surviving from ancient times. Patrick had labored for decades as a priest and bishop on this island at the end of the world — labored, in spite of constant threats of slavery and death, to bring a new faith to a people beyond the realm of the crumbling Roman Empire. He also faced harassment from church officials abroad who thought him inadequate to the task and were perhaps jealous of his success. In spite of these difficulties, he succeeded in bringing a new way of life to the Irish people. Today millions around the world remember him every year during celebrations on St. Patrick's Day.

Yet what is he remembered for? Driving the snakes out of Ireland, entering contests to the death with pagan Druids, using the shamrock as an aid to explain the Trinity — all these are pious fictions created centuries later by well-meaning monks. The true story of Patrick is far more compelling than the medieval legends. This story is known best from two short letters written by Patrick himself, his *Letter to the Soldiers of Coroticus* and *Confession*.

That we possess these two remarkable documents at all is the result of Patrick being forced in his later years to write, first, a letter of appeal and condemnation to a slave-raiding king and his band of mercenary pirates and, second, a defense of his work against accusations by fellow churchmen. Though Patrick wrote neither of these letters as history or autobiography, they contain fascinating and precious bits of information about his own life as well as about Ireland during a turbulent age. The two letters are in fact the earliest surviving documents written in Ireland and provide us with glimpses of a world full of petty kings, pagan gods, quarreling bishops, brutal slavery, beautiful virgins, and ever-threatening violence. But more than anything else, they allow us to look inside the mind and soul of a remarkable man living in a world that was both falling apart and at the dawn of a new age. There are simply no other documents from ancient times that give us such a clear and heartfelt view of a person's thoughts and feelings. These are, above all else, letters of hope in a trying and uncertain time.

The details that Patrick gives us of his life are few and often tantalizingly vague, but what we do know is this: He was born a Roman citizen in Britain in the late fourth century A.D. His grandfather was a priest, and his father was both a Christian deacon and a Roman decurion, an important local magistrate. He received at least a basic education in Latin, as would any son of the Roman upper class. As a teenager he committed an unnamed sin so horrendous that it almost destroyed his career decades later in Ireland. Soon after this sin, at the age of fifteen, he was kidnapped by Irish pirates from his family's villa in Britain near a place named Bannaventa Berniae, transported across the Irish Sea, and sold into slavery along with many of his family's servants. For six grueling years, he watched over sheep day and night for a single master. He experienced a gradual but profound spiritual awakening during these years as a slave. This awakening included visions and warnings that he believed came directly from God and that would continue throughout his life. He escaped from Ireland on a ship of pagan sailors and eventually made his way back to his family in Britain.

Later he returned to Ireland to spread the Christian gospel and was made a bishop. He preached in areas that had not previously known any missionary work, and he had many converts, including the sons and daughters of Irish kings, but many of his flock seem to have been female slaves. He experienced enormous difficulties, including threats, kidnapping, robbery, and other violence. At some point in his later years, a group of his newly baptized converts were killed or taken into slavery by a petty British king named Coroticus, prompting his *Letter to the Soldiers of Coroticus*. Also later in his life, he was accused by his fellow churchmen in Britain of corruption. He vigorously refuted these charges in his *Confession*.

But the letters of Patrick are not the only sources available for uncovering the story of his life and times. Archaeological excavations and discoveries shed a great deal of light on Roman Britain and early Ireland. Greek and Roman writers, although they never specifically mention Patrick, are marvelous aids in fleshing out the world he lived in. Later Irish traditions on Patrick, though full of legendary material, also preserve bits and pieces of genuine information. Taken together with his letters, these sources tell the story of an extraordinary man living in a tumultuous age.

One

The Early Years

My father was Calpornius, a deacon of
the Church, and my grandfather was
Potitus, a priest. His home was the village of Bannaventa Berniae, but he also
had a country estate nearby.

Patrick was born in Britain during the
closing years of the fourth century, probably
during the reign of the Roman emperor
Theodosius (347–395). His family was part
of the landowning aristocracy of the island,
an elite who controlled both the wealth of
Britain's agricultural production and the
power of local government, as well as the
high offices of the emerging Christian
Church. Patrick's Latin name, Patricius, in
fact means "noble, of the patrician class" —
the group who had ruled Rome ever since
Romulus and Remus legendarily founded
the city a thousand years earlier.

Patrick's father was Calpornius, a
common name in Roman Britain, and his

grandfather was Potitus. Potitus was probably born early in the fourth century, during the days of Constantine the Great, the first Christian emperor of the Romans. Potitus was a priest, but at this time in Christian history such a role was no impediment to marriage and children. His son Calpornius followed in his father's religious footsteps and become a lower-ranked member of the clergy, a deacon. It's likely that the motivation for both men taking holy orders was not purely or even primarily spiritual. The tax burden on wealthy Romans in the late Empire was heavy, so that many sought exemption by joining the clergy. The responsibility for collecting these imperial taxes fell on the *decuriones* or city councilors, of whom Calpornius was one. Aside from onerous revenue duties, the life of a decurion was one of honor and privilege. He was entitled to wear a purple stripe on his toga and could not be subjected to the degrading punishments faced by less fortunate citizens. The position of decurion was also hereditary, so that Calpornius must have smiled when he looked on his newborn son, knowing that he too would one day rule as part of the Roman nobility.

Patrick says his family estate was near

the town of Bannaventa Berniae, the location of which is unknown. Common sense tells us that if he was captured near there by Irish pirates, it must have been in the western part of Britain, close to the sea. There was a Roman town named Bannaventa in southern Britain, but it lies over seventy miles from the nearest port. The town of Glannoventa in northern Britain on the western coast would be perfect — fairly isolated, just a few miles inland — but for it to be the place we would have to assume the name was somehow miscopied as the manuscripts of the *Confession* were handed down over the centuries. Many other possible identifications have been made, but short of an archaeologist stumbling across a stone slab carved with the town's name, we will never know exactly where Patrick lived.

Britain had been part of the Roman Empire for more than three hundred years. By the fourth century, the native British were not the oppressed people yearning for freedom whom the Roman historian Tacitus describes in the first century A.D. In later years Patrick proudly called himself a *Romanus*, a Roman, and his fellow nobles at least also took pride in their Roman heritage, citizenship, and civilization. But the Romanizing of Britain had been slow and difficult.

Late in the summer of 55 B.C., the British warriors, skin painted blue, were waiting patiently on the beach for Julius Caesar. He was in the middle of his long campaign to bring Gaul, roughly modern France, under the power of Rome. He had just enough time before winter set in to make a dash across the Channel and punish those Celtic tribes who had been aiding his Gaulish enemies. Caesar knew little about the island of Britain — or Albion as the ancients named it — and less about the fighting ability of its inhabitants, but he decided to risk a quick invasion, sure that he could rapidly crush the troublesome British. It was almost the last mistake he ever made. The Roman invasion fleet with its heavy transport ships stalled in the shallow water off the beaches of Dover, forcing the legionnaires to leap into water up to their necks, fully armed and battered by the waves. The natives swarmed in on horseback and hacked the soldiers to bits as they struggled ashore. The British even used chariots in fighting — something the terrified Romans had only heard of from old tales of the Trojan War. Caesar eventually gained the upper hand after heavy losses, but Rome's first experience in Britain ended in a hasty withdrawal and only a brief foray the following year.

No Roman army visited Britain again for almost a century. Augustus consolidated the Empire, followed by Tiberius, Caligula, then Claudius. Far from the fool he is often portrayed as being, Claudius was an extremely intelligent and able emperor. In A.D. 43 he judged the time right for a second try. Four legions crossed the Channel and quickly overran southern Britain, moving in methodical Roman fashion into the central lowlands and much of Wales over the next fifteen years. The Roman troops who conquered Britain were given land there at retirement as a reward for their services and as part of the Romanization process. Tribal lands were confiscated, heavy taxes were imposed, and natives were forced to contribute to Roman temples, such as the temple of the imperial cult at the veteran colony of Colchester.

In the year 60, the spark needed to fan their smoldering resentment into a blazing revolt was ignited. Queen Boudicca of the Iceni was whipped and humiliated while her young daughters were raped by Roman agents bent on annexing her tribe's territory. The furious Iceni rose up against the Romans and persuaded surrounding tribes to do the same. Colchester fell to the British in a bloody massacre, and the rebels soon butchered those Romans foolish enough to remain in London. In the end relentless Roman efficiency defeated Boudicca and her army, though guerrilla warfare against the Romans continued in southern Britain for years. Beginning in 77, the Romans under General Agricola conquered the remainder of Wales and moved north into Scotland, beating the Picts at the climactic battle of Mount Graupius in 84. Agricola seriously considered conquering Ireland during these campaigns. He believed just one legion would be sufficient for the job and even kept an Irish king in his retinue just in case a puppet ruler was required — but the troops were always needed elsewhere. The Romans eventually withdrew from the Scottish highlands and, like the Chinese, built walls on their northern frontier to keep the barbarians at bay.

Peace descended on Britain for the next two centuries. Agriculture thrived, with perhaps 90 percent of the population living on farms. Gold, silver, and lead were exported to the continent, and British-born soldiers were a mainstay of the Roman legions. In the middle of the third century, while the rest of the Empire almost crumbled from revolts and invasions, Britain remained relatively quiet. The Saxons occasionally threatened the southeast coast, prompting a series of forts along the North Sea, but for the most part Britain was a calm if slightly backward island on the edge of the Roman world. In the 360s, however, a series of attacks from the Picts in the north, Saxons in the east, and Irish in the west created havoc across Britain. Walled towns were usually safe from the raiders, but farms were vulnerable. The invaders were gradually driven off with little lasting damage. Men like Patrick's father, Calpornius, may well have seen action against the Irish, called Scotti by the Romans, and told chilling tales to their children of the savages from across the Irish Sea.

Patrick's childhood days were divided between his family's house in town and the nearby villa. Bannaventa Berniae was probably a typical small settlement with fewer than a hundred houses laid out in a neat grid of crisscrossing streets. Many of the towns of Britain had grown from Iron Age Celtic villages that were transformed by the Romans into fortified settlements. Even the largest towns, such as Roman London or Colchester, couldn't compare with the enormous cities along the Mediterranean basin, but a traveler from Rome or Antioch would have found comforting familiarity in the layout of a provincial British settlement.

Patrick's hometown would have extended no more than a few hundred yards from end to end. As with every town, especially in the troubled days of the fourth and early fifth centuries, there was a sturdy wall enclosing the entire area with guard towers spaced regularly on top. A forum or town square was the center of social life and served as a busy market space. It was also the setting for any special events, such as the occasional visiting theatrical troupe — lighthearted, bawdy mime was a favorite; serious drama didn't play well outside the major cities. A bathhouse was a standard part of every town and was serviced by a sophisticated aqueduct system. The town house of Patrick's family, as did most Roman homes, probably faced inward along the street, presenting only a bare wall and door to the passing crowd.

Some homes were a single story, but many would have had a second floor used as sleeping quarters and private rooms. At the center of the house was often an open courtyard, providing light to the inner part of the home and serving as a gathering place for the family during good weather.

A temple to the imported Persian god Mithras may have been located inside the walls of Patrick's town. The secretive, male-only cult of Mithras had many followers among the army veterans, who were initiated by bathing in the blood of a slaughtered bull. Roman deities such as Mars, Jupiter, Mercury, and Minerva had their shrines in every town, as did native Celtic gods like Teutates, Maponus, and Brigantia. Outside the walls of the town were burial grounds for members of all religious groups. There families would deposit the ashes or bones of their loved ones. To read the many ancient inscriptions surviving from these British tombs is to glimpse the life and sorrow of real people. Mortality was high among infants and children in the ancient world, so that most families, even those of wealth such as Patrick's, would have known the pain of losing at least one child. A Roman inscription from York tells an all too common story:

To the spirits of the dead and to Corellia Optata, age thirteen . . . I, Quintus Corellius Fortis, the father of an innocent child, who prayed to the gods in vain, weep and mourn her with the deepest sorrow.

In the fourth century, small churches begin to appear in British towns, both inside and outside the walls. Patrick's family and the other Christian residents of the town would have been proud of their contributions to a prominent local church.

Bannaventa Berniae certainly served as a commercial center for agriculture in the area. Numerous small farms and a few larger estates such as that of Potitus and Calpornius would have been within a few hours' walk. The villas of Roman Britain, like the towns, would not have made much of an impression on an urbane visitor from the heart of the Empire, but they served their purpose well enough for the local nobility. Archaeologists have found that many villas were built on the sites of earlier Iron Age homes. This makes perfect sense as the basic needs for a reliable water supply, a location central to the surrounding fields, and protection from the elements were unchanged from Celtic to Roman times. In fact, aside from the occasional imported imperial official, many of the occupants of British villas would have been descendants of the same Celtic nobility who fought the Romans. Patrick's family may well have told stories of an ancestral British chieftain who had battled the legions three hundred years earlier.

A villa was first and foremost the heart of a working farm. A typical British villa would have consisted of various buildings laid out on three sides around an open courtyard measuring perhaps fifty yards across. A few villas in Britain were small palaces, but Patrick's country home was probably more modest. The main house would have contained several rooms and stood at one end of the courtyard. In this building were the sleeping and living quarters of the villa's owner and his family, along with the bedrooms of any domestic servants. Next to this building was often a small bathhouse with heated water — nothing like the facilities available in town but large enough for a small household. On either side of the main building were multiple barns and storage sheds for carts, horses, dried grain, and wool awaiting sale at the market, as well as sleeping quarters for the slaves who worked the fields. Many villas had large, decorated dining rooms and beautiful mosaics on the floors as marks of their owners' wealth. Scenes from classical literature were popular on mosaics and would not have seemed out of place to even the most devout Christian. In the first centuries of Roman rule, every villa would have made room for a shrine to a favored god or two. Patrick's family probably converted this emblem of traditional Roman piety into a small Christian chapel.

Patrick must have enjoyed his time at the country villa. A typical estate was surrounded by green fields and hundreds of grazing sheep. Britain was famous for its excellent wool, which was frequently used for winter cloaks. Patrick grew up watching the birth of spring lambs and the milking of cows, along with the harvest and drying of wheat. Not that he would have performed such chores himself — these were, of course, the work of slaves.

What language did Patrick speak as he grew up? A better question would be, Which of the many languages current in Roman Britain did he know? Latin was the spoken and written language of government, literature, and education, as well as the everyday language of many Roman soldiers and bureaucrats stationed around the island. From the time of Agricola three hundred years earlier, it had also been enthusiastically adopted by the upper classes of the native British. To the Celtic nobility, Latin was an essential tool for maintaining power under Roman rule. The British language, a Celtic tongue related closely to the language of Gaul and more distantly to Irish, was spoken throughout the island aside from the Scottish highlands. In those mountains the unconquered tribes clung to their native Pictish long after the fall of Rome. The Roman government never had an official policy of forcibly replacing native languages with Latin, so British continued to thrive under Roman rule. Few of the common farmers would have spoken Latin well if at all. Even in major cities such as London, British was widely spoken, and most of the population would have been bilingual to some degree. Unlike the native languages of Gaul and Spain (aside from Basque), British survived the end of Roman rule to evolve into the Welsh language still spoken today.

Patrick would have heard other languages as well from visitors and merchants in town. Many businessmen were Greeks, while in the later Empire soldiers were often of German origin. Slaves came from all over the Roman world. Those on Patrick's farm may have included speakers of Aramaic, Germanic, Pictish, and especially Irish. Irish natives captured in raids or wars would have been a convenient source of slave labor for Britain, and Patrick probably heard Irish spoken at the villa and in town from his earliest days. But the Irish in Britain were not just slaves. Many colonies of Irish expatriates — settlers invited in and granted land by the Romans in exchange for their service defending the coast against their hostile countrymen — existed on the western coast of Britain.

Patrick almost certainly spoke British as his first language. He writes in his letters that even in his later years he struggled with Latin. But like any member of the Roman nobility, he would have studied Latin from childhood and been expected to use it at school and when any visiting magistrate came to dinner. Depending on the native speech of the slaves surrounding him, especially the women who raised him, he may have picked up bits of other languages as well. It's likely that Patrick knew at least a little Irish from family slaves before he set foot in Ireland.

One amusing piece of evidence for Patrick's native language comes from an unexpected source. About two hundred years after the death of Patrick, the seventh-century Irish biographer and churchman Muirchú records a phrase that may go back to Patrick himself. The story goes that one Sunday when Patrick was trying to rest, he was disturbed by a group of noisy pagans. He ordered them to be quiet, but they just laughed. In his anger he blurted out *Mudebroth!* This word makes absolutely no sense in Latin or Irish, but as an old British phrase it would have meant something like "By God's judgment!" The surest way to discover anyone's native language is to listen to him when he's really angry.

Patrick grew up in a world rich with stories and colorful tales. From the time he could sit on his mother's knee, he would have heard stories of Greek and Roman heroes such as Hercules, Jason and the Argonauts, and crafty Ulysses. Aesop and his animal fables were as popular in Patrick's time as they are today, as was the famous story of the country mouse and the city mouse told by the Latin poet Horace. But even though Patrick was a Roman and an heir to a great classical tradition, the stories he heard from his family and household servants drew on a much wider background, reaching deep into Celtic mythology.

The native British preserved many of their ancient stories throughout the Roman occupation and into the Middle Ages. These were finally written down by Welsh scribes in collections such as the *Mabinogi* and even preserved in disguise in the lives of saints. By looking at these Welsh tales and carefully stripping away the later classical and Christian influences, we can see, however dimly, the kinds of Celtic stories in circulation in Patrick's day. Giants, monsters, heroes, magic — all these and more were part of the stories he would have heard. Tales of young warriors who overcome great odds to win beloved brides from their reluctant fathers are found all over the world, including ancient Britain. Celtic stories of arduous voyages to unknown lands to find the magical cup of healing, later the holy grail, were also a standard part of any storyteller's repertoire. Supernatural caldrons that could restore life to slain warriors, giants who could walk across oceans, poets who could change into animals to flee evil witches — the young Patrick would have heard about all of these as he sat beside the hearth fire during cold, windswept nights at the villa.

Patrick's formal education probably followed the standard Roman model. All instruction in classical times was privately funded and took place in groups, except for children of the wealthiest families, who could afford individual tutors. The first stage of a young Roman's education began at about age seven with instruction in the basics of letters and sounds, followed by the fundamentals of writing and simple mathematics. Many elementary teachers were ex-slaves with low social status and correspondingly low pay. School began at dawn, with discipline strictly enforced. A few softhearted teachers used honey-flavored cakes in the shapes of letters to teach their pupils the alphabet, but most preferred the painful motivation of a wooden rod. Some girls attended schools, but the vast majority of students were boys. Patrick would have gone to school in town, walking each morning to a small rented room near the marketplace with his erasable wax tablet and stylus in hand (papyrus from Egypt was too expensive). At all stages of their education, students from Christian families like Patrick would have had the additional burden of religious studies at the local church or at home.

At about age twelve, students moved to the second stage, studying language and poetry. Much of the day was spent reciting Latin verses — Virgil's *Aeneid* was a favorite of instructors, if not students — followed by explanation and analysis from the teacher.

The third level of a Roman education involved learning the all-important skill of public speaking. At this stage, from fifteen to twenty years of age, the basic skills learned in the earlier levels were perfected by the well-paid teacher. To a young man with any hope of a public life of government service, military leadership, or a role in the Christian Church, this level of training was essential. It was this final stage of education, as Patrick painfully points out in his letters, that he missed during his years as a slave in Ireland:

I don't have much education compared to other people. I was not able to study both literature and theology year after year as they did. They never had to

41

learn to speak any new language but could steadily improve their own Latin until it was practically perfect. But I write Latin as if it were a foreign language — any reader can easily see what kind of education I had.

Whatever attempts Patrick made in later years to improve his situation, he deeply felt the loss of those final years of formal education at Bannaventa Berniae.

Like many young people raised in religious households, Patrick rebelled against the faith of his parents. He was likely baptized as an infant, a standard practice since the mid-third century, and confirmed in the faith as a young man after years of instruction. Patrick knew the biblical stories of Joseph and his coat of many colors, Daniel's miraculous escape from the lions' den, and Jesus walking on water — he had also learned enough theology and church history to pass as a faithful son of a clergyman. But in his heart he cared nothing for religion. He was, as he admits, an atheist from childhood.

This lack of faith manifested itself when he was fifteen on the day he committed a sin, so shocking and horrible that it haunted him for the rest of his life. Even after his escape from Ireland, it weighed on his soul so heavily that he felt he had to confess it to his best friend to ease his conscience. After a lifetime of service in Ireland, the sin was still so damning that when it was made public by the same best friend, Patrick's fellow bishops in Britain wanted to put him on trial and strip him of his rank.

What could a fifteen-year-old boy have done that could ruin his life even when he was an old man? In his own *Confessions*, Patrick's elder contemporary St. Augustine bewails the boyhood sin of stealing pears from a neighbor's orchard, but Patrick's transgression was clearly in an entirely different league. Early Christian writers list three types of sins as the most severe for baptized Christians — sexual immorality, idolatry, and murder.

Sexual sins were any kind of sexual relationship between unmarried partners, including adultery, fornication, and sodomy. They were seen not so much as evil in themselves but as indications that a Christian had surrendered control of his or her body to fleshly gratification rather than to God. For those who willfully committed such sins, penance was rigorous. Patrick says his sin was committed during "one day in my youth — not even a day but in an hour." A roll in the hay with some willing slave girl at the villa would fit this description. Still, even in our day of religious and public figures commonly being called to answer for sins of their earlier lives, the most narrow-minded critics are reluctant to bring up an opponent's teenage sexual escapades. The British bishops who wanted to discharge Patrick may well have been ready to seize on any excuse they could find, but a fifteen-year-old's brief sexual fling was not the ammunition they were looking for. Enough of them probably had similar skeletons in their own closets.

Patrick's secret sin could have been sexual, but a more likely choice is idolatry. We know by his own admission that Patrick cared little for Christianity in his youth, and there were plenty of other religious options in Roman Britain for a curious and rebellious youth. In the cult of Cybele and Attis, known from several sites in Britain, particularly devoted young men would castrate themselves to better serve the goddess. Other imported eastern cults such as those of Mithras and of Isis required less extreme devotion but would have involved acts guaranteed to scandalize any good Christian family. There were also plenty of native Celtic cults still thriving in Britain. A silver coin donated to a willing priest of Nodens or Epona would have gained Patrick admittance to any number of pagan ceremonies.

Murder in the ancient world and in the early Christian era was as great an evil as it is today. It was a presumptive act of taking on oneself the power of God over life and death — and the ultimate betrayal of loving your neighbor as yourself. As in Judaism, exceptions were made for killing in a just war or when an agent of the state was acting to punish a serious crime, but murder was never excused. It may seem at first that murder was an unlikely sin for a young man such as Patrick, but it fits very well with his description of a deed committed in only an hour and is one thing serious enough to endanger his career decades later and haunt his conscience even after his years of brutal slavery in Ireland. Patrick was fond of biblical parallels and surely knew the story of the young Moses slaying an Egyptian for beating a Hebrew laborer. For his crime Moses was driven into exile. Patrick likewise could have boiled over in anger at some provocation or unjust act and killed someone.

We will never know exactly what Patrick's great sin was, only that he never tries to deny it or diminish its seriousness. But whatever his feelings of guilt as a fifteen-year-old, he would have had little time to reflect on the deed in peace — life as he knew it was about to come to an abrupt end.

Two

Slavery

After I came to Ireland I watched over sheep. Day by day I began to pray more frequently — and more and more my love of God and my faith in him and reverence for him began to increase.

The professional slave raiders who came for Patrick were cold, calculating businessmen — they viewed their captives not as people but as merchandise. Even during the raid on Patrick's villa, they were reckoning how many would reasonably fit in their boats, which women would fetch the best price, and who among the men were too troublesome to risk transporting. It was a cold-blooded triage based on simple principles of supply and demand — those captives who would yield the most profit for the venture were spared while the rest were killed. They must have looked at Patrick and seen a good risk — young enough to be easily dominated but old enough for heavy labor. Any elderly men and women would have been killed outright, as would any infants and young children. There was simply no market for them where they were heading.

The heavy slave chains fastened around the necks of Patrick and the rest were designed for control, not comfort. About three feet of iron links separated one captive from another as they marched to the boats in small groups. One can barely imagine the emotional state of the prisoners — shock at being awakened in the middle of the night by barbarians who threw them on the ground and bound their hands painfully behind their backs, horror and grief at watching their friends, parents, and children slaughtered in front of them, and a dawning realization that their lives had suddenly, horribly changed forever.

Patrick says, "I was led away as a slave to Ireland as were so many thousands of others." He doesn't mean just from his villa of course, or even those taken during one season of raiding in Britain, but that he was in the company of countless souls. The irony is that most of these captives would already have been slaves working on estates in Britain. But slavery among the harsh but civilized Romans must have seemed far preferable to a life of servitude among the barbaric Irish. Even for those captives who were themselves Irish and heading home from slavery in Britain, return to their native island was a small comfort. Unless by some miracle they were bought by a kind member of their own tribe — and there were dozens of tribes in Ireland — they had little chance of seeing their families again. An Irish master felt no more brotherly love for an Irish slave from a different tribe than he would have for a captive Persian.

Patrick's journey across the Irish Sea took no more than a day or two, depending on his destination. The slavers were probably heading for one of the islands or peninsulas on Ireland's east coast, on which archaeologists have uncovered plentiful evidence of trade between Ireland and Britain. The modern bird sanctuary of Lambay Island just off the coast north of Dublin has yielded numerous artifacts suggesting a lively trade across the Irish Sea. The same holds true for the nearby Drumanagh Promontory, as well as Rathlin Island off the northeast coast. Wherever they were going, Patrick and the other fresh captives must have gazed fearfully at the green hills drawing ever closer.

Patrick at least would have known the stories of Ireland told in Greek and Roman books. The classical world had known about Ireland for centuries, but the reports were often vague, more myth than fact, and usually terrifying.

The earliest description of Ireland is pleasant enough and comes from Greek and Carthaginian sailors who visited the northern seas as early as the sixth century B.C. A late Latin poem called the *Ora Maritima* preserves a garbled account of these voyages. Starting from the islands off the northwest coast of France, the verses say:

It is a two-day voyage from here to the Sacred Isle, as the ancients called it. The island lies rich in turf amid the waves of the ocean. There the Hierni dwell.

Why Ireland was called "sacred" is a something of a mystery. It may have been because distant islands in the west were traditionally supernatural or simply because the native name for Ireland sounded much like the Greek word *hiera,* meaning "holy." The *Hierni,* or Irish, who lived there were known, even at this early date, to burn turf for fuel in their homes as was commonly done until the last century.

Centuries passed before anyone else from the Mediterranean wrote of Ireland, but these reports are far from flattering. The first-century B.C. Greek Diodorus Siculus says its inhabitants eat human flesh, while a few decades later the geographer Strabo claims that Ireland is a frozen island on the edge of the world. He adds that the Irish are cannibals who eat their dead fathers and shamelessly have sex with their own mothers and sisters. He also notes that they are horrible gluttons. We should take this and other reports with a large grain of salt, because Strabo admits he has no proof and because such slander of distant foreigners is standard in authors from the earliest Greek historians to Marco Polo's medieval accounts of central Asia. Descriptions of Ireland and the Irish improved slightly by the mid–first century, when the Roman Pomponius Mela writes that Ireland is perfect for growing grain and so rich in sweet fodder that cattle left to graze unrestrained would literally explode from overeating. However, he adds that the Irish natives themselves are crude barbarians.

The campaigns of Agricola in Britain during the latter part of the first century A.D. prompted his son-in-law Tacitus, a historian, to write that nearby Ireland was frequently visited by Roman merchants. As for the character of the Irish people, he simply states that they are much like the British. The Greek geographer Ptolemy in the next century wrote a detailed description of Ireland's coasts and rivers, along with the names of sixteen Irish tribes, such as the *Woluntioi,* who feature as the Ulaid tribe of the epic hero Cú Chulainn in medieval Irish saga. Ptolemy knew the Shannon River (*Senu*) in the west and the Boyne (*Buwinda,* "white cow" in Irish) in the east near Tara. As Dublin wasn't founded until the Viking era, it isn't on his list of ten settlements, which does include *Regia* ("royal") and *Dunon* ("fort").

Around the year 200, the Roman author Solinus composed his *Collection of Amazing Facts,* the supermarket tabloid of the day. In it he writes that the warlike Irish enjoy draining the blood of their slain enemies and smearing it on their own faces. He also recommends using imported Irish dirt as an insecticide and notes — two hundred years before Patrick — that there are no snakes in Ireland.

The Irish raids on Britain in the 360s were carefully noted by contemporary historians such as Ammianus Marcellinus. He writes that the Irish broke peace treaties and ravaged the frontiers of Roman Britain, terrifying the inhabitants for years. Ammianus says the Irish even raided beyond Britain, presumably all the way to Gaul. There, in the late 360s, a young man named Eusebius Hieronymus, better known to history as St. Jerome, reports that he ran across Irish savages and saw with his own eyes how they would cut the nipples and buttocks off unlucky shepherds and their wives and eat them as a special treat.

All these stories must have gone through Patrick's mind as he approached Ireland. He would also have known about Roman trade with the island because Bannaventa Berniae stood near the Irish Sea. Tacitus was right that the Mediterranean world knew the ports and harbors of Ireland well. Irish archaeologists have found numerous early Mediterranean artifacts, such as Etruscan figurines, Egyptian beads, and even a Barbary ape skull, on the island. By the first century A.D., there seems to have been a brisk trade in fine Roman pottery and especially wine from Gaul, which continued until the end of the Roman Empire. At the ancient Neolithic tomb of Newgrange, north of Dublin, researchers have unearthed numerous Roman coins that seem to have been left as offerings by visiting merchants. There is even evidence of writing in Ireland from this early date — part of a broken gold torque from Newgrange was inscribed by a literate visitor with Roman letters sometime during the first century A.D. This sacred site on the Boyne River frequently plays a part in Irish mythological tales of the otherworldly Tuatha Dé Danann, or fairy people, and was undoubtedly an important religious site for the early Irish and any visiting Roman businessmen wishing to curry favor with the local people.

There are also buried hoards of treasure in Ireland that confirm the accounts of Irish raids on Britain. Over two hundred ounces of silver ingots from the time of Patrick's youth were unearthed together near Derry in the north of Ireland. Some of the silver is stamped with Christian symbols and, coincidentally, with the abbreviated Latin phrase *Ex off Patrici,* "from the workshop of Patrick." Another hoard of Roman silver from County Limerick in southern Ireland has yielded similar Christian treasures.

The Latin language was probably spoken by some of the Irish long before Patrick and Christianity arrived on the island. The Roman Empire, especially nearby Britain, was a powerful commercial and cultural influence on Ireland beginning in the first century A.D. Some Irish sailors and merchants would have learned at least enough Latin to converse with Roman traders arriving in Ireland and to use on their own visits to Britain and Gaul. We know that the Irish language borrowed a number of terms from Latin at a very early date, especially words related to trade items imported from the Empire. The Old Irish *fín* (wine) and *corcur* (purple dye), for example, are not native Celtic words and probably derive from the Latin of Roman merchants.

Sometime in the fourth or fifth century A.D., an enterprising Irishman educated in Britain or Gaul even invented an alphabet for Irish based on the Latin grammar books used by Roman schoolchildren such as Patrick. This writing system, known as Ogam, consists of notches and lines carved on the edge of a standing stone. It was a poor alphabet for literature or poetry, but it was perfect for short inscriptions marking the graves of the dead. Memorial stones for deceased ancestors, another early borrowing from the Romans, still dot the landscape of southern Ireland, naming the dead from those early days in Ogam letters.

Patrick arrived in Ireland along with the survivors from the villa and was quickly sold. All we know for certain is that he belonged to a single master throughout his six years of slavery. Later Irish tradition says the man was a Druid named Miliucc, but such traditions also say Patrick had fingers that glowed like fire and raised giants from the dead. More likely his master was an ordinary farmer who needed a compliant young man to do the boring and thankless jobs his own sons avoided.

Where exactly Patrick lived during his time has been hotly debated for over a thousand years. Religious devotion, local pride, and coveted tourist dollars all rest on the thinnest bits of evidence. In truth, no one knows where Patrick tended his sheep. County Antrim near Belfast has long been a favorite choice, but this traditional location runs into one glaring problem from Patrick's own *Confession*. He says that when he escaped he journeyed almost 200 Roman miles — about 185 modern miles — to find a ship to carry him home. If Patrick were watching over his flocks on a mountain in Antrim, he could have seen his native Britain across the narrow North Channel on a clear day. It makes little sense that he would have traveled so far from his ultimate destination to find a ship. A better answer comes from working backward — if Patrick had to walk 185 miles to catch a ship to Britain, he probably was on the west coast of Ireland. A hint of where this might have been comes from the first vision Patrick recounts years later, after his arrival home in Britain. He says that he heard voices from near "the woods of Foclut near the Western Sea" begging him to return to Ireland. We may be reading too much into the text, but it makes sense that those asking him to return to Ireland would be from the only place he had lived on the island. The only clue to exactly where Foclut might be on the Western Sea comes from one of the dubious sources mentioned previously — the largely imaginary account of Patrick's later journeys by the seventh-century Irish biographer Tírechán.

Foclut, according to Tírechán, was in County Mayo near the border with County Sligo, close to the modern village of Killala. This location near the Atlantic Ocean, far from Britain, fits the evidence from Patrick's letter perfectly. Moreover, Patrick says he prayed "through snow and frost and rain." Even today this part of County Mayo is one of the coldest and wettest spots in Ireland.

Slavery such as Patrick experienced was omnipresent in the ancient world. Perhaps a quarter of the population were slaves, depending on the time and place. Very few people in Greek and Roman times were bothered by the idea of one person owning another. The Greek philosopher Aristotle wrote that some people were simply meant to be slaves, while others were meant to be masters. Unlike in the modern world, slavery was never based on skin color, but certain ethnic groups, such as Germans and Jews, were considered by many others to be natural slaves.

A person could enter a life of slavery through several avenues, including war, kidnapping, birth into a slave family, or even selling of oneself or one's children to pay a debt. Once a slave, a person was without any civil or legal rights, completely subject to the whims of the master. This included the power of life and death — no one would complain if a master crucified a particularly troublesome slave, though such actions were rare because slaves were expensive. Slave owning was not restricted to the rich, and many poor freedmen who had bought their way out of slavery prided themselves on owning a slave. The best position for a Roman slave was as a domestic servant. Household slaves might become practically part of the family, beloved by the children they raised, cared for in old age by their masters, or able to buy their freedom after a few years, though not all slaves desired to do so. Craftsmen slaves had a harder lot but still could hope for a decent life and perhaps freedom through hard work. Slave workers in the fields were even lower in the social order, but the worst fate for a slave was the backbreaking and deadly work in mines, such as those in Spain, which devoured human life on a grand scale.

The coming of Christianity did little to ease the lives of Roman slaves. Many Christians were slave owners themselves who didn't hesitate to use harsh punishments. With the Christian focus on a world to come, the lot of a slave was seen as temporary and external to the more important spiritual life. Although masters and slaves might worship side by side, slaves were always urged to remember their place and be obedient to their earthly owners. St. Augustine saw slavery as ultimately the result of the sin in the Garden of Eden that created an imperfect world, but he also railed against those slave raiders in his native Africa who kidnapped and sold Christian women and children abroad.

Slavery in pre-Christian Ireland was similar in many ways to servitude in the Roman world. Irish slaves were at the bottom of the social scale, subject to the same legal restrictions as children or insane people, but enjoying no rights whatsoever. Slaves were treated as simple property, so that if any stranger injured or impregnated a slave, he had to compensate the master, not the slave. In early Christian Ireland, attempts were made, often in vain, to forbid the use of a female slave by a master for sexual purposes, but in pagan times there were no such restrictions. As in the classical world, slaves in Ireland formed a substantial minority of the population and were central to the economy.

The female slave or *cumal* was the standard unit of currency in this precash society and was equivalent to three milk cows. Female slaves were used largely for domestic tasks, such as grinding grain and making bread, while male slaves performed menial jobs on the farm, such as herding livestock and chopping wood. Unlike in the Roman Empire, slaves were rarely freed and could not usually buy their way out of servitude. In fact, Irish law implies that freeing a slave threatens the natural order and could lead to misfortunes such as crop failure and milkless cows.

The Irish farm on which Patrick served for six years was primitive compared with his family's Roman villa. The entire circular homestead would have been no more than thirty or forty yards in diameter, surrounded by a fence of sharpened wooden poles standing on a raised ring of earth. A gate allowed access to the buildings inside and to the pens in which the pigs, cattle, and sheep were kept during the night. The main dwelling house was a large, round structure made of interwoven twigs and branches plastered with mud or clay to keep out the winter wind. The roof was a high, cone-shaped structure of reeds rising to a steep point to shed the almost daily rain showers. Near the large building were smaller structures, used for housing grain, equipment, and servants. Patrick didn't realize it, but the Irish farm where he now lived was almost identical to that of his Celtic ancestors in pre-Roman Britain. In coming to Ireland he had stepped back in time almost four hundred years.

Patrick's daily life at this time was determined by the seasonal rhythms of an agricultural land. He says that he cared for sheep during his slavery, such work being below the comparatively glamorous tasks of herding cattle and even keeping pigs. The ancient Irish were a cattle-based society, much like the Masai of eastern Africa, so prosperous farmers simply went by the name *cattlemen*. Horses and pigs were also highly valued animals, but sheep were definitely low-class. Every respectable farmer would have a flock or two for necessary wool production, but their care was the job of small children or slaves. Every day, rain or shine, summer or winter, someone had to lead the sheep out to pasture and lead them back again into a protected enclosure at nightfall. Wolves were still at large in early Ireland and preyed especially on young lambs.

Every spring in March or April, Patrick would watch through the night while the lambs were born. He then would help with castrating most of the young males and slaughtering them in the autumn for meat. At the start of each summer, Patrick would shear the sheep for their fleece, which the women of the household and female slaves would process into wool for clothing.

Patrick would have been familiar with all these tasks from his days at the villa, but he never actually had to participate in them before becoming a slave. It must have been humiliating at first for a young Roman nobleman to serve as a shepherd. He likely had other menial jobs as well, but care of the sheep was his primary task. Much of the time he was alone, moving the sheep from one field to the next as they ate the grass down to stubble. Many summer nights he would have passed in a small hut next to a stone-walled sheep pen in the hills. But more often he would have been at his master's homestead helping with chores and sleeping with the other slaves in a small shed. For a young man who had probably never even shared a bedroom and who once had slaves at his own disposal, it was certainly a change in lifestyle.

Even though Patrick scarcely realized it at

the time, all his experiences as a slave on an Irish farm were training for his future career. Every day he picked up more of the language, so different and yet similar in many ways to his native British. He watched and listened and learned to keep his mouth shut except when he had something important to say. He became familiar with the customs and gods of a foreign land. Not least of all, he learned to look beyond his own immediate desires to care for the needs of his flock. He had to guide them and watch over them, to see that they had enough food to eat and protect them from wolves. It was good practice. As he says:

God used the time to shape and mold me into something better. He made me into what I am now — someone very different from what I once was, someone who can care about others and work to help them. Before I was a slave, I didn't even care about myself.

As the years in Ireland passed, something began to slowly change inside Patrick. He had laughed at the priests in Britain behind their backs and rolled his eyes with his friends during the church services he was forced to attend — but now, with the cold wind biting his face and the never-ending rain soaking his skin, the idea of a God who loved and cared for his own took on a new appeal. A cynic might say that a desperate person will grasp at any hope, real or imaginary, but others would say that, as with Jonah in the belly of the great fish, it often takes a true calamity for someone to pay attention to a God who was always there.

Patrick says he was once "like a stone stuck deep in a mud puddle, but then God came along and with his power and compassion reached down and pulled [him] out." He began to remember the biblical stories and prayers he had learned in his childhood, reciting them over and over. Patrick says that he would get up before sunrise and say a hundred prayers every morning, with another hundred every night. Since prayer in the ancient world was usually out loud, the other members of the household, free and slave, must have noticed this change in his behavior. In a later vision, Patrick would hear the Irish calling him "holy boy," probably a derisive nickname earned at the farm because of his endless prayers. The pagan Irish, just like the Romans, prayed to their gods to fulfill specific needs. Religion for them was a business relationship — you sacrificed a sheep to Mars or Lugus, and in return you got help with your crops or cursed a rival suitor with impotence. No one went around praying constantly. The gods wanted sacrifices, not endless ramblings of devotion.

Patrick says he also began to fast at this time. Fasting was a prominent feature of Jewish religion and was taken over by Christians, who regularly abstained from food during holy days and as a means of penance for sin. For Patrick, it was an act of purification and payment for the sins he had committed in his youth. But to the Irish fasting must have seemed a very peculiar form of religious activity. In Irish culture fasting was undertaken to shame a person you believed had done you wrong. If a neighbor had stolen your cow and refused to return it, you simply sat yourself in front of his house from sunrise to sunset, fasting for the whole tribe to see. No one could withstand this sort of social pressure long, and most grievances were quickly resolved. To his Irish owners and fellow servants, for Patrick to fast as a means of devotion to his god rather than as a complaint against him was completely topsy-turvy. They must have thought the boy had lost his mind.

Three

Escape

> But I soon ran away and fled the master
> I had served for six years. I left trusting
> in God, who took care of me on my
> journey, and I wasn't afraid — at least
> until I came to the ship.

For six long years Patrick labored in the woods and pastures of Foclut near the Western Sea. His early misery and resentment had changed with his growing faith into, if not happiness, at least an acceptance of his circumstances as the will of God. Perhaps he remembered from his childhood the New Testament passages that urged slaves to be obedient to their masters. Surely Patrick did his best to obey his master, but it must have seemed to this man, now in his early twenties, that the wretchedness of his life would never end. The friends of his youth back in Britain by now must have been thinking of marriage and children, taking responsibility for family businesses, making their marks in the world. And where was he? Stuck on some Irish hill at the edge of the world serving as a slave — a slave! He, Patrick, son of Calpornius, grandson of Potitus, a member of the Roman nobility. Even after six years, countless hours of prayer and fasting, and with an ever-growing faith in a divine plan, the reality of his situation must have seemed bitter indeed.

One night, as Patrick lay sleeping, he heard a voice speaking to him in a dream: "You have fasted well — soon you will be going home." One can imagine him waking with a start in his small, dark hut. In the ancient world, pagans and Christians alike believed in dreams as means of divine communication. Socrates dreamed of his forthcoming death, Cicero wrote of the possibility of prophetic dreams, and night visions from the healing god Asclepius were central to the diagnosis of disease. The Celts themselves believed that their departed relatives could speak to them through dreams and would spend the night at the tombs of famous ancestors hoping for visions from the dead. Patrick would also have remembered the biblical stories of God speaking through dreams to Jacob and Daniel. The dreams of Joseph led him to slavery in Egypt, but his ability to interpret such visions set him free.

But how could Patrick escape? It would be risking death to flee his master. No one would help him — no one would dare, even if sympathetic to his plight. Even a Druid or king would by Irish law have to return an escaped slave to his owner. And even if Patrick could make it to a nearby harbor, there were no ships to Britain from the west coast of Ireland. All the ports with ships departing for Britain or Gaul were on the north, south, or east coast. If he could somehow get to one of them, no captain or crew would risk their lives and their livelihood by helping an escaped Irish slave. It must have seemed ridiculous to Patrick — a dream of foolish hope rising from his own despair. Surely God would never expect him to do the impossible.

The next night, as Patrick slept, he heard the voice again: "Behold, your ship is ready." The voice even told him where to find the ship. Patrick must have awoken in utter shock. Once may have been wishful thinking, but to hear the voice of God twice — well, to him it had to be real. And he could not ignore the voice of God.

Patrick knew, as a Christian, that his duty was to remain faithful to his master, which certainly didn't include running away. But since God had given him a direct order, his conscience was clear. Still, the practical difficulties he faced were enormous. He would have to avoid contact with everyone, moving only at night, and then far away from settlements. He could take enough food with him to last a week or two at most, so he would have to supplement his supplies with berries, nuts, and any fish he could catch in the numerous lakes and streams. He couldn't steal food from any farm — not only would doing so be risking discovery but the voice had not given him permission to break any of the Ten Commandments. Fortunately for Patrick, it would have been summer, as ships could not sail the stormy seas around Ireland during the winter months. The overwhelming problem, however, was not supplies but the distance involved. The voice had told him the boat was waiting in a harbor two hundred Roman miles away.

Patrick was in the wrong part of Ireland for an easy escape. The archaeological evidence for Roman commerce with Ireland and Irish contact with Roman lands points overwhelmingly to a focus of trade in the area around Dublin Bay, Tara, and the Boyne Valley in the east, as well as the coast north of present-day Belfast and some trade along the southern coast and rivers. Patrick could have stood on the cliffs of northwest Ireland staring out at the Atlantic Ocean until he was an old man and never set eyes on a ship sailing for Britain or Gaul. Even the topography made escape difficult. Ireland is shaped like a bowl, with hills and mountains along its coasts and an often marshy interior crisscrossed by countless rivers and streams draining the rain-soaked center of the island. Early settlers built narrow wooden roads to cross the treacherous bogs, but even so, archaeologists regularly unearth the remains of unfortunate travelers who strayed from a safe path. The ancient Greek merchant Philemon reported that from east to west, it took twenty days to cross Ireland, a distance of roughly 150 miles. Perhaps he was recounting hearsay, but more likely he knew from personal experience the difficulties of traversing such sodden land.

The only destination possible for a fugitive journeying 185 miles from the northern coast of County Mayo would be a harbor in southern Ireland, such as Cork, Waterford, or Wexford. Patrick gives no hint of the location, only the distance traveled.

And so, one night soon after his second vision, Patrick made his escape. Under Irish law he was now an *elúdach*, a fugitive, in the same class as a wandering thief or murderer. But unlike a criminal, who might have relatives to shelter him or offer compensation to those wronged, Patrick was utterly alone.

Patrick's journey south could not have covered more than five or ten miles a day. He probably paralleled the river Moy at first, up between the Ox Mountains of County Sligo to the east and the Nephin Beg Range to the west. After a few days he would have reached the headwaters of the river Suck, leading him down night after mud-covered night through the countless bogs of the Central Lowlands to the Shannon River. Perhaps he crossed the Shannon, his biggest obstacle, near the future site of the great Clonmacnoise monastery. He might have taken off his clothes, wrapped his few dwindling supplies as tightly as he could, and swum across at a point that looked shallow and slow.

As Patrick moved south from the Shannon, the land would soon have become firmer and mountainous but cooler at night. He couldn't risk a fire, but to a young man who had spent six years in one of the wettest, coldest regions of Ireland, this last stretch over the Slieve Bloom Mountains down to the southern coast would have been tolerable. Depending on his final destination, he may have followed the river Nore. At Stonyford, on the western bank of the Nore north of Waterford, archaeologists have discovered a classic Roman cremation burial dating from perhaps the second century A.D. This probably indicates a long-term Roman presence in the area, perhaps a trading post selling Mediterranean wine and fine pottery to the tribes of Leinster. If the post was still active in Patrick's day and he knew of it, he must have been sorely tempted to seek refuge there. However, any Roman merchant with an ounce of business sense would never have offended his local customers by harboring a fugitive from Irish law, even a young Roman nobleman.

Patrick made his way down to the sea at Waterford or some southern port with active trade across the Irish Sea. He probably sat hidden in the trees watching the harbor until darkness fell before he made his move. This was the most dangerous part of his journey, the point where Patrick says he began to be afraid. He didn't look so different from any poor farmer in from the hills, but his imperfect Irish and foreign accent would have immediately given him away as a fugitive slave. Anyone could then have hauled him off to the local king and probably collected a nice reward, but Patrick knew he had to take his chances soon.

The next morning he surely prayed with all his might before working up the courage to approach a nearby ship preparing to depart with the tide. He approached the ship and spotted the captain issuing last-minute orders to the crew. The sailors were all pagans, Patrick reports, so they probably were Irish rather than British or Gaulish merchants, but at this date there were still many Romans who followed the old religions. Whether in Irish, British, or Latin, Patrick then made the simple request that would determine his fate — he asked if he could join the ship's crew. He had no money, of course, so offering his services was his only hope for passage. After six years of hard labor outdoors, he should have been a strapping young man, but his fasting combined with a monthlong trek across Ireland with little food must have worn thin the flesh on his bones. The savvy captain sized up the situation in an instant. He had a hundred things to finish in the next hour and didn't need a runaway Irish slave to complicate his life. He had neither the desire nor time to turn the lad in, so as Patrick says, his response was curt: "Forget about it — there's no way you're going with us!"

Patrick must have been dumbstruck as the captain walked away. He had believed the dreams and trusted in God to rescue him from slavery, to lead him to this very ship, yet here he was in a worse position than ever. There was no way home to Britain, he certainly couldn't return to his former master, and he had no desire to spend the rest of his days hiding in the Irish bogs. He says he turned back to where he had slept the night before, praying as he went. Suddenly he heard a voice behind him. It was one of the sailors shouting: "Come back quickly, we want to talk with you." Patrick returned to the ship and faced the captain yet again. The man was still surly, but he offered Patrick a position on the crew.

Why did the captain change his mind so quickly? Some might say that Patrick's prayers had been answered, but a more practical answer lies in old-fashioned greed and self-interest. Crossing the seas was a dangerous life, and sailors were never easy to come by, so any halfway fit man looking for work was not to be rejected lightly. Also, as Patrick says, the ship was departing almost immediately. If at the last minute they took aboard a runaway slave, who was to know? If inquiries were made next time they were in the port, they could always shrug their shoulders. Fugitive slave? Patrick? Never heard of him. The best part of the deal for the captain would be that, after he had worked the young man nearly to death hauling cargo, he could resell him into slavery at any foreign port, even in Britain. There were plenty of British-born slaves working in the tin mines of Cornwall. Since Homer's time every other slave claimed he was really of noble birth, tragically kidnapped in his youth by cruel pirates. No one would listen to Patrick's story.

One quick business matter had to be taken care of before casting off — Patrick says the sailors asked him to suck on their breasts. This short phrase in his *Confession* has struck readers as so utterly bizarre that medieval scribes even tried to change the text to say something else entirely, but "suck their breasts" is clearly the original reading. What could this possibly mean? Some scholars have suggested that it is merely a colorful metaphor indicating friendship, which echoes certain passages in the Old Testament. However, it is best taken as it stands — the sailors expected Patrick quite literally to suck on their breasts. This is not quite as strange as it seems, since in stories from that of Hercules in Ancient Greece to Algerian folk tales in modern Africa, for an adult to suck another's breast, even between males, is a common form of adoption and bonding. In a medieval tale, a dwarf at the mercy of the Irish king Fergus mac Léti sucks his breast as a token of submission and friendship. Whatever we may think of the practice, Patrick writes of it in an offhand way, clearly expecting his readers to be familiar with it. The sailors saw it as a simple ritual for joining the crew — they had all done it and expected anyone else wishing to become one of their number to do the same. Still, Patrick considered it a pagan practice and proudly says he refused because he feared God. The sailors were apparently in too much of a hurry to quibble, so as Patrick writes, "I climbed up on the ship, and immediately we set out to sea."

It must have been a great relief for Patrick to see the green hills of Ireland fading over the waves. He doesn't say exactly what the ship's destination was, only that it was a three-day voyage. With a fair wind, the ship might have made it all the way to Gaul in three days, landing on the western coast of Brittany. But the voice had told Patrick he was going home, so it seems reasonable that Britain was their goal. A leisurely three-day voyage across the Irish Sea could have taken the ship anywhere from Cornwall to southern Scotland.

Patrick's description of what happened after landing is extremely odd: "For twenty-eight days after that we wandered through empty country." Britain is a large island, but a month's travel could take an energetic trekker over a very large area. And how could the land be deserted? Ever since Caesar, the two constants in describing Britain have been its rainy weather and its dense population. And why didn't the ship just land at one of the busy ports on the western side of the island? There are no clear answers, but there are several possibilities. Either the ship foundered unexpectedly or the captain deliberately put ashore in an empty region. Perhaps the seas were rougher than the crew could handle, or perhaps they were being pursued by pirates and decided to save their cargo by beaching before they reached their intended harbor. Why was the land empty? In Patrick's day Roman roads and towns barely reached into some sections of coastal Britain, such as Cornwall, Devon, and the Cambrian Mountains of Wales. A ship's crew carrying supplies and cargo on their backs could easily have spent a month of aimless wandering in such areas before finding a decent-sized settlement. We will never know for certain. To Patrick, what matters and what he records from this personal exodus from a land of slavery are his own spiritual trials in the wilderness. Throughout the narrative Patrick is clearly emphasizing for his readers the parallels between his escape and the flight of the children of Israel from bondage in Egypt.

Here he describes events about two weeks into their trek:

We didn't have any food, and hunger was making everyone weak. The next day the captain said to me: "Well, Christian, what are you going to do? You say this God of yours is so great and powerful — why don't you pray to him for us? We're dying of starvation here! I don't think we'll ever see another living soul again." But I answered him with great confidence: "Just turn with your whole heart to the Lord my God, because nothing is impossible for him. Today he's going to send food right into your path — plenty to fill your bellies — because his abundance is everywhere." And by the help of God that's exactly what happened.

Just as the starving Israelites had ridiculed Moses in the wilderness of Sinai, the captain mocks Patrick and his Christian God's inability to feed them. Patrick responds with great confidence, but instead of quail and manna the sailors stumble on a large herd of pigs crossing the road in front of them. Pork was a favorite food among the Celts, so Patrick's prayers could hardly have yielded a more pleasing meal. He says the sailors killed many of the pigs and had a feast that lasted two days. His fellow travelers, Patrick notes, also looked on him with new respect. He then adds, as an aside, that the dogs traveling with them were also well-fed at this time. This is an odd statement, which has stirred much debate. Why would there have been dogs onboard a merchant ship? Why wouldn't the sailors just have eaten the dogs if they were starving? The answer is simple — the dogs were part of the cargo. There is a revealing contemporary letter in which the Roman senator Symmachus, one of the last defenders of the old religion, describes to his friend Flavianus the arrival of seven huge Irish dogs in Rome for use during public games. Their size so astonished the crowd that they believed the dogs must have been brought in iron rather than wooden cages. The ship that carried Patrick must have been on the first leg of a journey to transport such dogs on their way to festivals and games in Britain or for further shipment to the continent.

Pigs were not the only bounty for the hungry men. As Patrick says:

> They even found some wild honey at one point and offered me a share. But then one of them said: "We've dedicated this as a sacrifice to the gods." Thank God I found out, because then of course I ate none of it.

Once again Patrick had an opportunity to demonstrate to the sailors — and to his readers — that he scrupulously avoided anything associated with pagan religion.

Just after refusing the honey, Patrick had a peculiar and frightening experience:

That same night as I lay sleeping, I was attacked by Satan — an event I will remember for the rest of my days. He fell on me just like a huge rock so that I couldn't even move my arms or legs. Somehow it came to me at that moment, even in my ignorance, to call on the prophet Elijah for help. So as the sun began to rise, I shouted out with all my might: "Elijah! Elijah!" And as the rays of the sun touched my body, immediately all the weight and pain were lifted away. I believe that it was Christ the Lord who rescued me that night and that it was his spirit which cried out for my sake.

This sudden nocturnal paralysis evoked a cry in Patrick that he believed emanated from the spirit of Christ himself. The Old Testament prophet Elijah barely figures in modern Christian thought, but this was not so in early Christianity. In the New Testament he appears with Moses in the transfiguration of Jesus. To the Church Fathers he prefigured the life and work of Christ as well as his resurrection. He was also a popular figure on early Christian sarcophagi, standing in his fiery chariot ascending into Heaven. These representations are particularly interesting because they are clearly modeled on similar images of the Greek and Roman sun god Helios ascending in his own chariot into the sky. In early Christian thought, and at least unconsciously in Patrick's mind, images of Elijah (*Helias*) and the sun (*Helios*) blended together so that the rays of the rising sun lifted the demonic weight from his limbs.

The rest of the journey was uneventful and even pleasant. Patrick reports that they traveled ten more days with plenty of food, warm fires at night, and oddly enough for Britain, good, dry weather. Patrick saw the provident hand of God still caring for them — the very day they ran out of food, they arrived at a settlement and were safe at last.

Four

Home

So after many years, I finally returned home to my family in Britain. They took me in — their long-lost son — and begged me earnestly that after all I had been through I would never leave them again.

If ever there was a prodigal son warmly welcomed home by a loving family, it was Patrick. No one taken by Irish raiders had been known to return alive. No one had ever escaped from Ireland. His family had mourned him as dead, which they assumed he was. If he hadn't been killed or died on the way to Ireland, they believed he must have perished after six years of slavery among a savage people. When Patrick walked through the gate of the villa near Bannaventa Berniae one afternoon in autumn, it was as if a ghost had returned from the land of the dead.

The man who returned to his home in

Britain was very different from the boy who had been stolen away. Patrick had been fifteen when he was kidnapped, but he was now twenty-one. He was taller, leaner, and stronger, with skin roughened by years spent out-of-doors. But the differences in Patrick's appearance were nothing compared with the changes that had taken place inside him. He had been a spoiled, self-centered teenager who cared about nothing but his own desires of the moment. He returned a man who had been through a profound psychological and spiritual transformation. Some of the maturity noticed by Patrick's mother and father would have happened over six years even if he had stayed in Britain, but there was something about Patrick now that went far beyond the inevitable setting aside of childish ways.

Consider what he had been through in the half dozen years since he had last seen his family. He had been violently ripped away from everything near and dear to him. He had seen murder and brutality up close. Pirates had carried him off to a distant land in which he was merely a piece of property. No one there asked him what his wishes were or how he felt — no one cared. For over two thousand days and nights, he did as he was told or he was beaten, like an animal. There must have been times as he stood with the sheep on the cliffs overlooking the Western Sea that he seriously considered throwing himself off to end his misery. What did he have to look forward to anyway? Marriage, perhaps, to some slave girl of his master's choosing, but he would then have to watch as his own children, who should have known joy and freedom instead of pain and servitude, suffered his fate. But something in Patrick made him endure; some small spark of life that had been with him all along kept him going through harder times than most of us could ever imagine. Then one day he escaped — a dangerous and daring journey. No one who had suffered Patrick's trials and overcome them as he did could return to Bannaventa Berniae the same person.

But not all of Patrick's experiences produced positive results. Again and again through his letters we catch glimpses of a man who was forever scarred by his experiences as a slave in Ireland, no matter how much he grew from them. Reading the words of an old man, we can still see a terrified boy huddled alone on a windswept hillside. Patrick eventually overcame his pain, but he never left it completely behind.

Patrick returned to a Britain that was trapped between two ages. The ancient world of Rome was fading away, yet the medieval world of Anglo-Saxon England had not yet begun. Roman Britain had taken more and more responsibility for its own rule since the invasions of the 360s. This "barbarian conspiracy" of Picts, Saxons, and Irish had ended only with the arrival of Count Theodosius, father of the future Roman emperor of the same name, who crossed the Channel in 367, driving out the marauding bands and rebuilding Roman fortifications. One of his lieutenants was a soldier named Magnus Maximus, who at first loyally defended the Empire. Patrick's father, Calpornius, may well have served with him in his campaigns against the Picts and Irish in the north during the early 380s. But in late Roman history, successful generals were rarely content merely to guard the frontiers. Magnus was declared emperor by his troops in 383 and took much of his army from Britain to Gaul in an effort to shore up his imperial claim. He was later defeated and beheaded, and his actions left

Britain weakened. Rome still governed, but defense and administration fell increasingly on local British noblemen.

In 402 the German-born Roman general Stilicho stripped Britain of even more Roman troops to fight barbarian invasions on the continent. Local councils of decurions such as Calpornius huddled together and debated what to do now that most of the legions were gone. They could raise some troops from their own British countrymen, but not enough to cope with any major incursions from abroad. They likely filled in the gaps in their forces by importing foreign mercenaries, as was common in the late Roman Empire. Germans were the most popular, but Picts and Irish could also be hired for the right price. This practice of using wolves to help guard the sheep worked only as long as the number of mercenaries was kept relatively low.

Patrick must have looked at the land he had returned to and wondered why the Roman Empire, which had ruled the world for centuries, was falling apart. Even though much of Roman culture and tradition would remain vibrant into the Middle Ages, something happened in the fifth century that caused the final collapse of imperial rule in western Europe. Many theories have been put forward to explain the decline and fall of the Roman Empire, from lead poisoning to excessive taxes, but the best answer lies in a combination of causes that came together during Patrick's early life. Some have suggested that Christianity itself was the problem. A religion that teaches its followers to turn the other cheek and love one's enemies, critics have said, does not encourage the sort of fighting spirit needed to resist the bloodthirsty barbarians pouring over the town walls. But there were no great pacifist movements in Christian Rome. Warriors went out to battle the Germans with the cross carved on their shields and hymns on their lips. And the Eastern Roman Empire, which if anything was more devoutly Christian than the West, maintained imperial rule against numerous invaders for another thousand years.

A better answer lies in the makeup of the Roman army and the pressure exerted by migrating tribes from the east. The Roman Empire of the fourth and early fifth centuries had become dependent on common soldiers and military leaders drawn from the very Germanic tribes that threatened the frontiers. These were not the simple

Roman farmers of earlier days who left their fields to defend their homeland out of love and duty. The mercenaries were well paid for their service — and if the silver coins weren't forthcoming one year because of a poor economy or political squabbling, they would not hesitate to rise up, declare their own emperor, and march on the centers of power to claim their due. This scenario occurred again and again in the West during the later Empire, with stability eventually being restored for a few years. But then the ferocious Huns from central Asia arrived in eastern Europe and began pushing the Germanic tribes westward in flight. There was no place for the Germans to go except into Roman lands, so in 406 the great movement across the Rhine into Gaul began. Roman power did not collapse all at once with the Germanic invasions, but there was a steady, relentless loosening of the emperor's grip on the western provinces.

All evidence points to a continuation of Roman-style rule in Britain even after the sack of Rome in 410 and the emperor Honorius's subsequent letter urging the Britons to look after their own defense. The Romans of Britain had largely been doing just that for several decades. During the years of Patrick's slavery and return, taxes in Britain continued to be collected, Roman coins from Gaul and Italy circulated, Latin was spoken, and decurions still wore their trademark purple stripes of the Roman nobility. Nevertheless, although the island Patrick returned to was still Roman in form and function, it was on the verge of tremendous changes. The trickle of foreign mercenaries would become a flood of Angle and Saxon settlers by the middle of the century, while the power vacuum created by the absent legions and overwhelmed town councils would soon be filled by a new breed of homegrown tyrants.

Patrick doesn't say how long he remained at home or what he did during that time. One can imagine the first few days were filled with joyous reunions with family and friends. Dinner after dinner with aunts, uncles, neighbors, childhood companions — everyone asking him to tell the story of his years in Ireland and especially his dramatic escape. For a time Patrick must have been quite a local celebrity. His parents especially must have been overjoyed to see him again. No one, save Patrick, could have suffered more than they during his years of slavery.

Many people undoubtedly offered advice on what he should do now that he was home. He had missed the most important years of his education, so his parents may have encouraged private lessons to make up for the lost time. Whatever he did, we know they begged him to remain at home. They wanted their son near after such a long separation, of course, but they also needed his help. Patrick never mentions brothers or sisters, so he may well have been an only child. In any case, his parents were growing older and would have needed him around the villa more than ever. There was always so much to be done — planting, harvest, construction, repairs, supervision of slaves. One wonders if Patrick looked at his own family's slaves any differently now.

Calpornius would certainly have had plans as well to groom his son as an up-and-coming official at Bannaventa Berniae. With the Roman central government gone, more responsibility than ever fell on the local councils, and a bright, hardworking young man could go far in the new Britain. Patrick's father must have regarded his son with pride and relief. Calpornius had probably despaired at his family's political and economic future without an heir to take over from him. Now, at last, everything would be all right.

Patrick's first vision was the strangest. As he lay sleeping in his old room one night soon after his return home, he dreamed he saw a man arriving from Ireland with a huge number of letters in his arms. The man, who said his name was Victoricus, walked up to Patrick and dumped the load on the foot of his bed. Victoricus then picked one letter from the top of the pile, broke the seal, unrolled it, and handed it to Patrick. As Patrick began reading, he saw that the heading of the letter said "The Voice of the Irish." An odd title for a letter, he must have thought. All of a sudden, he heard an enormous chorus of voices singing to him, and it seemed as if the sound were coming from the letter itself: "Holy boy!" they sang, using Patrick's mockingly given nickname while he was a slave among the Irish, "Come here and walk among us!"

Patrick says his heart was breaking as he read these words and, being able to read no more, he awoke. Why would he feel such sorrow at a dream urging him to return to Ireland? A more expected reaction

93

might be utter disbelief or even anger. Return to a people who had kidnapped him, sold him into slavery, brutalized him, and almost killed him? Part of the answer may be that Patrick's newfound Christian faith had created in him a genuine love for the Irish. "Love your enemies," Jesus says during the Sermon on the Mount. "Pray for those who persecute you." Another part of the answer may lie in the identity of Victoricus. Patrick never says who he is and never mentions him elsewhere. Later traditions turn him into an angel named Victor who ministered to Patrick in Ireland, but in Patrick's letter he is just a man. His name was a common one in the Roman world and is certainly not Irish. Some have suggested that Victoricus was an old friend of Patrick's from Britain, but why would such a man appear to Patrick in a dream *as if he were arriving from Ireland?* A better answer would be that he was a fellow Roman enslaved in Ireland, perhaps a friend Patrick left behind in the woods of Foclut. Whoever he was, his appearance and the pleas of the Irish in the dream deeply moved Patrick.

Patrick's second dream was very different. In this vision there was only a single voice. He recounts:

I heard the most beautiful words, a prayer — but I couldn't understand what was being said. Only God knows if the words were coming from inside me or were somewhere beyond me.

No one brings a letter to Patrick in this dream. In his mind, he had already received the call to return to Ireland — a divine plea from the Irish, not an order from God — so he was now struggling with an overwhelming decision. He must have prayed a great deal since the first dream, seeking some peace from God. Should he leave his family and the life he had yearned for through years of slavery? Should he really give up everything near and dear to him to return to a people who would probably kill him for his efforts? But his prayers were not working — he simply didn't have the words to express his anguish. At last, in his sleep, he heard a strange voice speaking in heavenly words beyond human understanding. In Patrick's dreamworld, the final words suddenly became clear: "The one who gave you your spirit, it is he who speaks in you." To Patrick, God himself was speaking inside him, praying the words that he had been unable to speak for himself. Patrick's reaction on awakening this time was not sorrow but joy.

To hear the beautiful angelic words, to know that God was working inside him gave him confidence that God would truly be with him.

He had to listen to the voices of the Irish calling him to return — no matter what his friends or family would say, no matter what he wanted for himself. He could not ignore this divine call, this awesome commission. Patrick was going back to Ireland.

Five

The Missing Years

> I am Patrick the ignorant sinner and, I declare, a bishop in Ireland — a position I believe I was appointed to by God himself.

It's easy to imagine the reaction of Patrick's parents when he told them of his decision to return to Ireland. They probably sat stunned, perhaps thinking it was some kind of joke. When they finally realized he was serious, they surely begged him to reconsider. To leave his family, to give up a prosperous villa, to abandon a promising political career, all for the sake of an island of hideous barbarians who had done nothing except cause pain to Patrick and those who loved him — unbelievable! Fine, become a priest if you must, they probably said, your grandfather Potitus did that, but he never left behind his wealth and position to run off and preach to savages. We'll even build you a chapel here at the villa, have services every day if you want. If you're looking for miscreants to convert, there are plenty here in your own neighborhood!

As much as Patrick loved his parents, he couldn't resist what he believed was a divine call to return to Ireland. But the years between Patrick's escape from Ireland and his return are a mystery. We don't know how long this period was or exactly what he was doing. However, Patrick couldn't simply pack his bags and return to Ireland as a freelance missionary. There was a set path to be followed if a man wanted to be a priest and work within the structure of the Christian Church. It would require great dedication and years of training.

Christianity was still a relatively young religion in the fifth century. Only four hundred years before Patrick, Jesus had been executed on the far side of the Empire, in the Roman province of Judaea. At first Christianity was just one of many sects within Judaism, distinguished only by its belief that Jesus was the promised messiah. These early Christians all continued to observe the Mosaic law and other Jewish practices such as circumcision while spreading their teaching in synagogues throughout the eastern Mediterranean.

But within a few years the new movement had attracted enough attention to rouse the displeasure of the Jewish hierarchy. A young rabbi named Saul was dispatched from Jerusalem to nearby Damascus to root out the Christians in the Jewish community there. On the way Saul experienced what he believed was a miraculous encounter with the resurrected Jesus and soon turned from Saul the persecutor to Paul the evangelist of Christianity. Paul then broke with the Jewish Christian leadership in a radical and far-reaching decision to spread the gospel to non-Jews throughout the Empire. With the destruction of Jerusalem by the Roman legions in the year 70, Christianity abandoned its Jewish roots and prospered in the Greek-speaking towns of Syria, Asia Minor, Egypt, even Rome itself.

The Christian movement began to attract the unwanted attention of the Roman government in the latter half of the first century. The Romans were always lenient toward native religions. As long as the locals paid their taxes and didn't cause any trouble, they were free to worship their ancestral gods. Rome insisted only on an additional token sacrifice to the emperor as a show of loyalty. Jews were exempted from this sacrifice and offered prayers for the emperor instead. While Christianity remained a Jewish sect, its members were also excused, but as soon as the new religion separated from its parent faith, it became suspect. The emperor Nero blamed the Christians for the great Roman fire of 64 to deflect suspicion from himself and had many in the Christian community at Rome, including Paul and the apostle Peter, killed.

Persecution of Christians continued over the next few decades, but only sporadically. There was no official policy regarding Christianity, and Roman governors were left to punish or ignore members of the religion at their own discretion. In 112, Pliny the Younger — best known for his description of the eruption of Mount Vesuvius, which buried Pompeii — was Roman governor of Bithynia in Asia Minor. He wrote the emperor Trajan seeking advice on how to deal with Christians in his province. Pliny describes early Christian worship from a Roman point of view:

They declare that on a certain day of the week they gather before sunrise and sing a hymn to Christ as a god. They also take a solemn oath together, not with any criminal intent, but swear they will never steal, rob, commit sexual sins, or cheat in business. At the end of this ceremony they depart but then meet again later for a harmless meal together. They claim to have ceased doing this when I issued my order forbidding secret societies. Still, I tried to discover the truth by torturing two female servants called deaconesses, but all I got out of these women were absurd and bizarre superstitions.

Trajan responded that Christianity was certainly an undesirable movement, but members of the group shouldn't be hunted down or persecuted unless they publicly refused to sacrifice according to Roman law. If they obstinately resisted, then they should be executed as examples to others.

In spite of these restrictions, Christianity continued to spread during the second and third centuries. Persecutions, when they occurred, were usually localized and short-lived. From the beginning, Christianity had a special appeal to women and to the lower classes, perhaps as a result of its emphasis on mercy and equality. It also grew and prospered more in the Greek-speaking East than in the Latin-speaking western part of the Roman Empire. Furthermore, Christianity was primarily an urban religion, so that rural areas, even in the east, were almost exclusively pagan even at the dawn of the fourth century.

In 284 the emperor Diocletian inherited an empire that was in a shambles — military revolts were commonplace, and barbarians were overrunning the borders everywhere. To reverse this downslide, Diocletian instituted a number of sweeping reforms, such as the separation of civilian and military powers, as well as a massive reorganization into new provinces. In 303 he turned his attention to shoring up traditional Roman religion in an attempt to unify the Empire. Christians were first on his list of troublemakers, so he began what became known as the Great Persecution. Diocletian (who oddly enough had a Christian wife) commanded that churches and sacred books be burned, clergy be imprisoned, and every last Christian offer sacrifice. This final persecution of Christianity ceased only when Constantine the Great attributed his victory in 312 over a rival just outside Rome to miraculous intervention by Christ. Even before this battle Constantine had tolerated Christianity, but afterward he became an outspoken advocate for the faith and ordered a return of all confiscated church property and freedom of worship.

By the end of Constantine's reign, in 337, Christianity was well on its way to becoming the dominant religion in the eastern part of the Roman world. But in the less populous and more agrarian West, evangelism proceeded much more slowly. Gaul is a case in point. When Irenaeus, bishop of Lyons, died in 202, he was probably the only bishop in all of Gaul. By the end of the third century, churches under the supervision of bishops were well established in several major towns, including Trier and Paris. Still, Christians were only a small minority of the population in late Roman Gaul and sent only one bishop to the famous Council of Nicaea in 325. In the countryside surrounding the Gaulish cities, a Christian would have searched far and wide before finding another member of his faith.

The Christian world in which Patrick grew up was torn by controversies. During the first three hundred years of the new religion, the external forces of Roman persecution and omnipresent worship of the gods didn't allow Christians the luxury of breaking apart into rival groups. There were always differences of course in what various Christian teachers declared to be the truest meaning of the Scriptures, but it was only after official acceptance of the church by Constantine that the disagreements lying just below the surface of Christian thought could rise to the surface. Foremost of these was the exact nature of Christ. Was he God become human, human become God, or some combination of the two? The Egyptian theologian Arius in the early fourth century proposed that God the Father and Christ were not identical in nature but that Christ, while being fully divine, was created by and subordinate to his father. This view was flatly rejected by traditionalists who saw God and Christ as an eternal, uncreated unity. After many heated arguments and not a little outright violence, the traditional view triumphed, at least officially, when Constantine convened the Council of Nicaea.

While such controversies may seem tedious to us, they were vitally important to Christians of the time. Some believed a Christ who struggled to obtain divinity was a model for all believers, while others thought the idea of God creating a son sounded suspiciously like the tales of

Greek mythology. The difference was also important to the larger political picture of Patrick's world. Many of the Germans who moved into the Roman West in the fifth century were not worshipers of pagan gods but fellow Christians who had been evangelized by disciples of Arius and were thus of a different theology than most of the Romans under them, who by and large adhered to a traditional view opposing Arius. There is little evidence of Arian sympathy in Britain, and Patrick's letters certainly stick to the orthodox theology, but Arianism was a close neighbor and potential threat to the church in the British Isles.

The distant isle of Britain had an even later start on the road to Christianity than did Gaul. Imaginative stories tell of Joseph of Arimathea from the New Testament traveling to Glastonbury, but the first Christians to arrive in Britain were probably Roman merchants in the late first or early second century. The early history of the British church is complicated by the fact that there are so few historical sources to draw on. Patrick's letters are in fact among the earliest and best evidence of British Christianity. We do know from scraps in Roman authors that Christianity had reached Britain by the beginning of the third century and that a few years later St. Alban became the first British martyr. A small number of British bishops attended a church council in Gaul in 314, suggesting a close and perhaps subservient relationship of the British church to the Gaulish leadership. Three British bishops traveled to Italy in 359 to take part in a church council attempting to solve the Arian controversy and later wrote of their opposition to the doctrine of Arius.

Archaeological evidence for Christianity in Roman Britain is slim, especially in the earliest centuries, but scattered artifacts do attest to the presence of Christian worship. A second-century inscription on part of a large vase was found at Manchester in 1868 with letters forming the words "Pater noster" (our father) in the shape of a cross. It's possible that this and similar graffiti had a pagan significance, but it's more likely they indicate a Christian presence in Britain just over a century after the crucifixion. More plentiful archaeological evidence from the later Empire confirms that Christianity flourished among the British elite, such as Patrick's family, during the fourth century. Artifacts include elaborate baptismal fonts, expensive silverware, and beautiful mosaics with Christian motifs, though the foundations of only a few early churches have been discovered in Britain so far. At Lullingstone, in southeastern England, a fourth-century chapel was decorated with Christian figures praying with arms upstretched to Heaven in a style found throughout the Mediterranean. Elsewhere in southern Britain are several Roman villas decorated with figures of Christ. The great hoards of buried silver with Christian images, similar to those found in Ireland, pose more of an interpretive problem. Were these riches stored in peaceful times or in fear of potential raids, perhaps by Irish pirates? Whatever the case, the great riches bearing Christian symbols buried around late Roman Britain clearly show that there were many wealthy Christians on the island.

Cremation was the most common form of burial in the Roman world, but it began to pass out of fashion in the later Empire, especially among Christians. On the southern British coast, in Dorset, archaeologists have found a fourth-century cemetery with numerous Christian burials. Most were simple graves facing east to await the resurrection, but more prominent local Christians indulged themselves with elaborate memorials.

★ ★ ★

In 429, probably during the time of Patrick's training, Bishop Germanus from Auxerre in Gaul made the first of two visits to Britain to combat a rising Christian heresy. This deviance from the accepted faith was associated with a Briton named Pelagius, born in the mid–fourth century. Like Patrick, Pelagius was the son of British nobility and received his education in Britain. By 390 he had left his island home and traveled to Rome as leader of a Christian reform movement. He and his comrade Celestius were in Palestine in 415 to defend what were seen by the Christian leadership as some very dangerous ideas, including a denial of the sinful nature of humanity and a belief that men and women could, at least in theory, live perfect lives without God. Augustine and Jerome turned the full and mighty power of their writings against Pelagius and his followers. Jerome, never one to shy from insulting an enemy, compares Pelagius to a terrified dog and calls him a mindless fool fat from eating too much porridge. It is interesting that Jerome twice calls him *Scotti*, that is Irish, in birth, though this is probably meant more as a vile insult than as a testimony of his origins. Pelagianism was repeatedly condemned in favor of more pessimistic views of human nature, but it was a heresy that refused to die, especially in Gaul and in Pelagius's homeland of Britain.

It's tempting to see Pelagius as a product of the same rough-and-ready frontier atmosphere in which Patrick was raised. Pelagius must have been a young boy during the devastating raids on Britain during the 360s. He grew up in a land that had always been on the edge of the Roman world and that was used to looking after itself when the central government ignored its frequent pleas for help. Such a setting could have encouraged a theology of self-reliance. But to southern Christians like Augustine, this was exactly the wrong response to a harsh world. We can admire the spirit of Pelagius and declare that Augustine was a killjoy who burdened Christian thought forever with the idea of original sin, but to contemporaries and to Augustine himself, the sinful nature of humanity was the great leveler of society. Pelagius and his followers argued that human nature was not so bad and that a few righteous and disciplined Christians might eventually gaze at the glory of God by their own efforts. Augustine said that no one was above anyone else — everyone, from the village prostitute to the most holy monk living a life of prayer in a desert retreat, was equally sinful and needed the unmerited grace of God.

There are no hints of Pelagianism in Patrick's letters. He came from an island full of the ideas of Pelagius, but Patrick seems to have followed the traditional Christian view that all human nature is sinful and in need of redemption. Patrick's position on the matter could have been shaped by training among anti-Pelagian bishops or it could have been a more personal reaction, based on the experiences of his own life. Repeatedly in the letters, Patrick emphasizes the overwhelming grace that he experienced at the hands of God. In his mind at least, the power of Heaven had personally reached down and rescued him not only from slavery but from a life of meaningless self-indulgence and emptiness. Patrick believed with all his heart that if the chasm between God and humanity was to be bridged, it had to be by the grace of God alone.

Patrick's Christian training during his missing years probably followed a steady progression up the ranks of the clergy, from layman to deacon, then priest, and finally bishop. Where did he receive his religious training? There were no seminaries to attend. Any man wanting to be a Christian minister had to study with a bishop and gain his approval before ordination. In some cases, as with Patrick's father and grandfather, this may have been a rather casual process, requiring only a minimum of time and effort. But Patrick was not looking to receive ordination to avoid taxes or lead a local church in his spare time. He had a much loftier goal in mind and thus needed the kind of training that would convince the bishops he could be given leadership of a mission to Ireland.

One of the early medieval sayings attributed to Patrick states:

I had the fear of God as my guide as I journeyed through Gaul, Italy, and the islands of the Tyrrhenian Sea.

The Tyrrhenian Sea lies off the Mediterranean coast of Gaul and Italy and is famed today as a vacation spot, but in Patrick's time one of the islands near the shore was home to the great monastery and teaching center of Lérins. Many leaders of the fifth-century church in Gaul were trained at Lérins, and commentators from the earliest times to the present have argued that Patrick studied there as well. Other stories say he went to study with Germanus at Auxerre, and it is conceivable that he did just that. If not Germanus, Patrick could have lived and studied in the household of some other Gaulish bishop in one of the cities or the newly established monasteries. But in Patrick's letters — our only reliable source for his life — he never mentions visiting Gaul except to dream wistfully of traveling there to meet with other Christians. Would Patrick have left Britain for training if he could have remained on the island? Maybe, if there were some compelling reason to seek a Gaulish education, but we have none in the letters. Our evidence for British Christianity is very limited, but we know there were British bishops present at London, York, Lincoln, and elsewhere on the island. It's unlikely that Calpornius and Potitus left their homeland for training, and family connections in Britain may have been crucial to Patrick's ordination. Since he had missed the last years of his education and lacked the Latin skills any other applicants would have possessed, family ties and influence were probably essential in Patrick's acceptance into the ministry. These ties would have been strongest in Britain.

We know from his letters that Patrick first became a deacon. In the early Christian church, a deacon was the lowest ranking member of the clergy and assisted bishops and priests in a wide variety of tasks. A deacon might administer charity to widows and orphans, serve as a messenger, bury the dead, and balance the church books. Female deacons existed but had a limited role, assisting in tasks involving their own sex, such as baptism and ministering to Christian women who were sick. A deacon would act as the eyes and ears of a bishop among the local congregations and could become very powerful if he earned the bishop's trust. Bishops in fact were often chosen from the ranks of deacons rather than from priests. The minimum age for ordination as a priest was thirty, so it's likely Patrick spent at least his twenties studying and serving as a deacon to a local British bishop. Even in an organization of equality and brotherly love, connections mattered, so Patrick must have worked hard to prove his worth and develop ties to bishops throughout Britain. He probably traveled among towns delivering messages while learning church finance, almsgiving, ministry to the sick and needy, and whatever else the bishop needed him to do.

The ordination ceremony on becoming a priest consisted only of a prayer by the bishop followed by a laying on of hands. Priests worked closely with bishops and were primarily responsible for teaching, baptizing, preaching, and administering the sacraments to congregations, much as Christian priests and ministers do today.

Advancement to the final rank of bishop in the early Christian Church was long and slow, usually at a minimum age of fifty. The particular role of a bishop no doubt depended on the region in which he served but included undertaking all the duties of a priest on a grander scale, as well as representing the local churches at larger council meetings. Bishops were chosen and ordained by at least three other bishops, but they had to be approved by the local congregations. Stories of wandering monks suddenly proclaimed bishops by local churches may be more fiction than fact, but no bishop could take on his office without the approval of the Christians whom he would serve. Certain bishops in major cities such as Antioch, Constantinople, and Rome had power and influence that stretched far beyond their local communities. The Pope, being bishop of Rome, exercised great influence, especially on the churches of the western Empire from before the time of Constantine, but it was only during Patrick's own lifetime that papal power became increasingly dominant.

Of all his duties and powers, it was the right to ordain clergy that was the distinguishing mark of a bishop — a power Patrick would have needed if he were to spread the gospel in Ireland.

The missing years of Patrick's life are so frustrating because we don't know exactly where he was or what he was doing. We do know he eventually became a bishop, but we don't even know when he achieved this position. If it was before he returned to Ireland, there was a gap of at least twenty-five years between his escape and his return. This seems unlikely for a man who had heard such a compelling call. It's much more likely that Patrick received his training as a deacon and priest in his twenties and early thirties, then soon returned to minister to the Irish.

Six

Return to Ireland

I came to Ireland to preach the good news. . . . I have had many hard times, even to the point of being enslaved again, but I traded in my free birth for the good of others.

The small boat carrying the first bishop of Ireland approached the rocky coast beneath the towering Wicklow Mountains south of Dublin Bay. The wind had carried them across the calm Irish Sea from Britain in less than two days. Two deacons gazed at the green hills before them with a mixture of excitement and trepidation, but their leader had a look of absolute calm and fearlessness in his eyes. The sailors quickly brought the craft to a nearby cove. As they pulled the boat up to the beach, the bishop probably took a deep breath of salty air and stepped out onto the shore. His name was Palladius.

One of our best sources for events in the fifth century is a detailed chronicle by a papal confidant named Prosper from southern Gaul. His entry for the year 431 says:

> Pope Celestine ordained Palladius and sent him to the Irish believers as their first bishop.

We can be sure that Patrick was not the first Christian to set foot in Ireland — he wasn't even the first bishop. Palladius had been a deacon like Patrick's father before being appointed a bishop, but unlike Calpornius he was an influential churchman who moved in the upper circles of power in Italy and Gaul. Palladius also appears in Prosper's chronicle under the entry for 429 as the man who arranged for Bishop Germanus of Auxerre to travel to Britain to combat the Pelagian heresy. We can picture Palladius traveling from Pope Celestine in Rome to Germanus in Auxerre, then across the Channel to Britain to lay the groundwork for the bishop's visit. He would have worked as an advance man with anti-Pelagian supporters in the British church. He must have been successful. Prosper says Germanus arrived and triumphed over the heretics, restoring the Britons to the true faith. Even when we grant that things may not have gone as smoothly as Prosper records, we can be sure that Palladius made a positive impression on Celestine during his British mission. Pelagianism had existed in Britain for several decades and was not about to be wiped out by a single visit from a Gaulish bishop, but this was an important start.

Sometime during or just after the visit of Germanus to Britain, a letter arrived on Celestine's desk from a group of Christians in Ireland requesting a bishop for themselves. Perhaps the letter was relayed by way of Britain from Germanus or Palladius. We know that the request came from the Irish because bishops were never sent anywhere unless there were already Christians living there who had requested a spiritual leader. The letter presented a unique opportunity to the Pope. The small Christian community in Ireland, if firmly guided by a bishop opposing Pelagian ideas, might act as balance against churchmen in Britain resisting orthodox views. The Pope could, in effect, outflank the Pelagians of Britain by encouraging a traditional church in Ireland. In any case, it was certain that if he didn't provide a bishop for Ireland, the Pelagians of Britain would seize the opportunity and send their own man.

When Celestine considered his candidates for bishop of Ireland, it must have been an easy choice. Palladius had proved himself a hard worker and loyal Christian during his recent mission to Britain. He had strong contacts with the anti-Pelagian forces among the nearby British bishops and good relations with the church in Gaul. He was immediately ordained and sent north to Ireland along with a support staff of priests and deacons.

One of the assistants who accompanied Palladius may well have been Patrick. The timing is right. Patrick would have been in his mid-thirties by 431 if he had been born in the late fourth century. He would have had several years of training and service as a deacon. But more important, Palladius would have needed someone who knew Ireland, its people, language, and customs. Patrick would have been a qualified, logical, and presumably eager choice.

But we know very little about the mission of Palladius or where exactly in Ireland he served. Later stories associate him with Leinster and southern Ireland, which makes sense because this was an area in frequent contact with Roman Britain. Roman merchant activity, shown by the number of Roman artifacts found in the south and the fact that settlers from this area had themselves planted colonies in western Britain, provided the necessary contacts for the introduction of Christianity to the island and for a Christian community to form there. Some of these Christians would have been native Irish, but many were probably slaves taken from Britain like Patrick. Whoever they were, the Christians of Ireland had requested a bishop, and Palladius was sent.

Later tradition says that Palladius failed miserably in Ireland and died in disgrace within a year, but these tales were written to make Patrick's success all the more spectacular. Medieval biographers such as Muirchú relate the story:

> Palladius, archdeacon of Pope Celestine, who was then bishop of Rome and forty-fifth in line from St. Peter the Apostle, was ordained and sent to this island in the frigid north so that he might convert it. But he was unable to carry out this task because no one can accomplish anything on earth unless it is granted by heaven. The wild men of Ireland would not listen to his preaching nor did he himself wish to remain here in a foreign land. He decided to return to Celestine, but after crossing

the Irish Sea, died in Britain during his journey home.

The Irish annals all give the same account — Palladius arrives in 431, fails immediately, and is replaced by Patrick in 432. The later Irish historians could not simply do away with Palladius as the first bishop of Ireland since the text of Prosper was too well known. They had to find some way to discredit and minimize his work so that the arrival of Patrick could shine forth as the true, divinely commissioned beginning of Christianity among the Irish. The annals even have Palladius building his few churches in wood rather than enduring stone. Poor Palladius was quietly pushed to one side over the next few centuries while Patrick became the island's patron saint.

In the Middle Ages several local churches in southern Ireland claimed that their founders also arrived before Patrick. These claims may be only local pride or they may preserve however dimly a bit of history. Such stories reflect a battle that raged between the northern church, at Armagh in Ulster, and other congregations throughout Ireland. Armagh claimed it was the rightful heir of Patrick, God's own apostle to the Irish, and therefore had supremacy over the other churches on the island. This leadership was not only spiritual and organizational but material. The mother church imposed certain financial obligations on the subordinate churches. Naturally enough, many churches in southern Ireland resisted what they saw as Armagh throwing its weight around. They countered that while Patrick may well have established Christianity at Armagh, there were saints working in their part of Ireland before he ever arrived. If this was true, then Armagh did not have priority over them. Names such as Ailbe, Declan, Ibar, and Ciarán are found in early accounts as missionaries to southern Ireland before Patrick's time. As always, we have to be very careful when looking at these later sources, but they may contain bits and pieces of genuine history amid the fantastic miracles and outright propaganda.

Of the tales concerning the supposed saints of Ireland before Patrick, that of St. Ailbe is particularly fun to read. Ailbe shares his name with a marvelous hound of mythology who guarded southern Ireland from encroachments — a not-so-subtle tweak at the northern churchmen at Armagh. The human Ailbe was associated with the town of Emly in southwestern Ireland, and his tale bears the marks of both Celtic mythology and traditional renderings of the lives of holy men. Like many good Christian saints, and unlike Patrick, he was of humble birth. Ailbe's mother was a slave whose son was magically raised, as were Romulus and Remus, by a wolf. Ailbe was later taken in by a kindly pagan and eventually baptized by none other than Palladius. After traveling to Britain, Gaul, and Rome, where he was warmly welcomed by the Pope, Ailbe brought Christianity to Ireland in the days before Patrick through miracles and wonders.

The stories of the saints before Patrick usually end with some sort of reconciliation, but there are a few tense moments. In the *Life of St. Declan*, Ailbe, Declan, Ibar, and Ciarán strenuously debate whether they should recognize the newcomer Patrick as their overlord. Ciarán and Declan immediately want to make peace, and Ailbe reluctantly gives in, but Ibar says he will never yield Ireland to some foreigner from Britain. When Ibar almost comes to blows with Patrick, an angel has to step in and make peace between the two saints.

Whenever Patrick arrived as a missionary in Ireland — whether it was with Palladius or later, as a bishop or as just a priest — the later sources all agree that the center of his work was in the northern part of the island, though we don't know exactly where. Patrick himself never says in his letters where he labored, except that he went "to the most remote parts of the island — places at the very edge of the world, places no one had ever been before."

Patrick was not the first Christian missionary to work in lands beyond the Roman Empire. Armenia was evangelized by the beginning of the fourth century, and the king of Georgia was converted soon after, reportedly by the miraculous work of a Christian slave woman. Also in the fourth century, a young Roman named Frumentius from Tyre, on the eastern Mediterranean coast, suffered a fate remarkably similar to that of Patrick. Frumentius and his brother Aedesius were returning on a merchant trip with their uncle along the Red Sea when they were attacked and captured by Ethiopians. Everyone but the two young men was killed, after which Frumentius and his brother were taken to Ethiopia as slaves. In time they rose to positions of power in the royal court and founded several churches. Frumentius later traveled to Egypt to seek a bishop for his Ethiopian converts and was appointed to the position himself. The Germanic Goths of eastern Europe were evangelized in a similar way at about the same time. Ulfilas, a slave of the Goths whose Christian family was from Asia Minor, worked ceaselessly among his captors and ministered to the enslaved Christian community. He was eventually appointed bishop and translated the Bible into the Gothic language — though he omitted the violence-filled Book of Kings from the final version so that it wouldn't rouse the passions of an already war-loving people.

Patrick's closest model as a missionary bishop may have been his elder contemporary Ninian, who worked to convert the Picts in southwestern Scotland. We know of Ninian only through later sources who say he founded a monastery at Whithorn on the Irish Sea, which became a center of evangelism. It's possible and very tempting to suppose that Patrick knew of and even studied with Bishop Ninian. At Whithorn, in the rugged hills just across the narrow sea from Ireland, Patrick would have had the perfect training ground for work among the Irish. In his *Letter to the Soldiers of Coroticus*, he seems to be particularly furious with Picts who had accepted Christianity, then slid back into their pagan ways. Perhaps they were a tribe he had worked with under Ninian and so he felt a personal disappointment and anger toward them.

Patrick's two letters tell us a good deal about his years of work among the Irish, even though he is short on geographical details. We know that he saw his role in Ireland as twofold — first, to care for Christians already present in his region and, second, to preach the Christian gospel to any pagans who would listen.

Patrick never says how large the Christian community was in the north when he arrived in Ireland, but a reasonable guess would be that there were hundreds of Christians scattered through the area, especially along the eastern coast, facing Britain. As with the south, some were probably free Irish, but the majority must have been Christian slaves brought from Britain. Most of these would have been women. With the help of the native Christian Irish, these Roman-born slaves must have gathered in whatever worship and prayer services their masters would allow. Some Irish slave owners would have forbidden their slaves access to other Christians and any visiting clergy, but many may have seen an advantage in allowing slaves to participate in a religion that urged them to be obedient to their earthly masters while looking toward a new life after death.

It's very likely that some Christian slaves were successful in converting their masters, as happened elsewhere beyond the borders of the Empire. But whoever these Christians were and however many of them lived in the north, they must have welcomed the arrival of Patrick. By the time he was an old man, we know that Patrick had a sizable Christian community under his care. Some were wealthy enough to offer him expensive offerings, which he always declined, but many were female slaves who owned nothing, not even themselves. Patrick says in his *Confession* that he couldn't bear the thought of leaving these poor women behind to travel back to Britain. This was probably sentimental in part but also practical, because he acted to the best of his ability with their Irish masters as a protector of these women. What little security they had in life may have depended on him.

But Patrick was more than a shepherd for his Christian flock. He had a compelling sense of mission to spread the gospel to new people and places on the island. He must have taken every opportunity to preach in areas of the north that had never heard the Christian message. He would have kept the details simple and straightforward — no hairsplitting theological debates, as were the fashion in Rome or Constantinople. After all, he was preaching to a people new not only to Christianity but to the very idea of a single God. The Irish religious world was inhabited by countless gods and goddesses, forces of sky, earth, and water, magical powers of ancestors and divine animals, reincarnation, and otherworldly beings. Christianity must have seemed dull by comparison to those Irish who would stop and listen to Patrick.

Patrick would never have worked alone during his Irish ministry. Even in the days before he became a bishop, he would have had clergy and others to help him with the many spiritual and practical tasks involved in a pioneering and often dangerous mission. His helpers were probably few at first, so Patrick likely pitched in with daily tasks when he wasn't off visiting distant Christians or preaching in new areas. We also know that he ordained clergy during his years as a bishop. He says as much in his letters and even mentions a particular young priest whom he had taught from childhood — for at least thirty years. The ordination of a native clergy would have been an essential step in spreading the gospel and in the survival of Patrick's work after his death.

The worship services Patrick conducted would have been plain by modern standards. Much of the time they would have been out-of-doors or in a small home, even a barn, as he traveled about the countryside. Any churches Patrick and his followers built would at first have been simple structures made of local materials and based on examples from Roman Britain. On Patrick's home island, early churches were usually unpretentious wood buildings. In the late Empire a few Christian communities in Britain built stone churches, but even these were chapels no more than forty feet in length. If Patrick in time gained the political and financial support to build a stone church in Ireland, it would have been similar to these. At the front of such a church, a priest would stand to read the Scriptures to the congregation, who were standing or sitting on rough-hewn benches. Also in front would have been a small altar on which the Eucharist was celebrated.

Dress for Christian ministers in the early centuries of Christianity was often no different from everyday clothing, but by the time of Patrick, priests had begun to distinguish themselves from their congregations, at least during worship. White clothes, such as bleached robes, were especially favored as symbols of purity and cleansing of sin. Since Druids also wore white, Patrick may have consciously used this color of clothing to mark himself as a religious practitioner. Otherwise, his appearance would have been plain and simple. Pope Celestine himself chastised certain Gaulish bishops for adding decorations to their vestments: "Clergy must be distinguished from the people they serve not by clothing, style, and refinement but by their teaching, speech, and pure minds."

A Christian worship service in Patrick's Ireland would have been similarly unadorned by modern standards. The congregation would have gathered together to hear the Scriptures, sing from the Psalms, and celebrate the Eucharist in imitation of the last supper of Jesus and his disciples. Patrick may have used Latin for some of the prayers and blessings, both for the British slaves present and to introduce his Irish converts to the language of the western church, but sermons would have been in the common Irish language.

We have a good idea of the basic message Patrick preached because in his *Confession* he gives a creed or summary of his beliefs. This statement, though fifteen hundred years old, is very similar to the words still recited by millions of Christians today:

There is no other God — there never was and there never will be. God our father was not born nor did he have any beginning. God himself is the beginning of all things, the very one who holds all things together, as we have been taught.

And we proclaim that Jesus Christ is his son, who has been with God in spirit always, from the beginning of time and before the creation of the world — though in a way we cannot put into words. Through him everything in the universe was created, both what we can see and what is invisible. He was born as a human being and he conquered death, rising into the heavens to be with God. And God gave to him power greater than any creature of the heavens or earth or under the earth, so that someday everyone will declare that Jesus Christ is Lord and God. We believe in him and we wait for him to return very soon. He will be the judge of the living and the dead, rewarding every person according to their actions.

And God has generously poured out on us his Holy Spirit as a gift and a token of immortality. This Spirit makes all faithful believers into children of God and brothers and sisters of Christ.

This we proclaim. We worship one God in three parts, by the sacred name of the Trinity.

Creeds were an important part of Christianity from the earliest days of the faith, though they were not put into a formal statement such as Patrick's until the end of the second century. These creeds were never meant as complete theologies, just as short statements covering the core of the faith.

What we know today as the Apostles'

Creed began in Rome in the early third century as a declaration by candidates for baptism. It spread throughout western Europe as an affirmation used by new Christians at this crucial ceremony — and it is no coincidence that Patrick's statement is so similar to it. The Apostles' Creed, or something very much like it, is the confession Patrick would have learned in Britain and later taught to his Irish converts. Christian creeds became more complex as bishops struggled to define precisely the human versus divine nature of Christ, but these debates held little interest for Patrick. He saw himself as a laborer in the fields of the Lord, not as a theologian.

We could ask, as many have, what exactly Patrick believed about a number of religious issues that were important to his contemporaries and later Christians. But Patrick's letters reveal little about his views on these controversies. His theology is simple and straightforward, and contains no surprises. What mattered to Patrick were not debates on the Trinity but the overwhelming sense of God's love and grace to humanity. This was the message he taught the Irish.

To understand truly Patrick's years of

work in Ireland, we need to look closely at those people who could have helped or hindered his mission the most: kings, who held the reins of political power in Ireland; Druids, the ancient religious order who stood to lose the most if Patrick succeeded; and women, both slave and free, who were his most loyal followers. We need to look back to a world completely foreign to us to see the role each of these three groups played. Patrick's own letters are crucial sources, but we must also use Irish law, ancient literature, and Celtic mythology to re-create the culture in which he lived and worked.

Seven

Kings

I used to make payments to the local kings. In addition, I also gave money to their sons who accompanied me on my journeys. But that didn't stop them from seizing me one time along with my companions. They were eager to kill me.

In the modern Western world, the individual is supreme. We hold it as a fundamental principle that all human beings are equal, even though we don't always live up to this ideal. In ancient Ireland, the notion that every person in society was equal would have seemed absurd. Early Irish culture was strictly hierarchical — everyone had a rank, from the lowest slave to the highest king, with legal rights depending wholly on social status.

As Patrick learned during his years of slavery, ancient Ireland was also a completely rural society. There were no towns or cities as in the Roman world, and there wouldn't be any until the arrival of the Vikings four hundred years after Patrick. The only community that mattered was the tribe, or *túath*. There were perhaps 150 of these scattered over the hills and valleys of Ireland during the fifth century. Within each tribe were a number of extended families, headed by a king. Given that Ireland is not a large island and that there were dozens of kings, we have to set aside any Hollywood images of medieval lords in giant castles ruling over vast stretches of land. An ancient Irish king was more akin to a Cherokee chieftain or a small town mayor than to King Arthur. Some Irish tribes ruled by these kings may have had several thousand members, but some would have numbered only in the hundreds. Each tribe was absolutely autonomous and formed a world unto itself. Alliances between tribes may have formed on occasion, and sometimes a particularly powerful king would have ruled as overlord of more than one tribe, but the rule of one tribe, one king, and outsiders be damned was the normal way of life in early Ireland.

The king had important duties within the tribe. He was the military leader and as such could summon all the able-bodied men at any time to defend the tribe's territory or to attack neighboring lands. The king would also regularly call an *óenach*, or assembly of the tribe, during which matters of religion, politics, or justice might be addressed — or for purely social purposes. These assemblies were often held on Celtic holy days, such as Lughnasadh in August or Samain in autumn, the ancestor of our Halloween.

An impressive example of an ancient Irish tribal assembly hall is found in the archaeological site at Emain Macha, just to the west of the town of Armagh in Northern Ireland. Excavations during the 1960s and '70s uncovered the foundations of an immense structure set on top of a hill in what must have been a royal fortress. The site had been occupied since the first farmers had arrived in Ireland, but some time in the last few centuries B.C., the hill apparently became the headquarters of the kingdom of the Ulaid, known from the epic *Táin Bó Cuailnge*. At the beginning of the first century B.C., a circular structure measuring well over a hundred feet in diameter was built on the hill. Inside this building were four concentric rings of posts leading to a central oak column reaching almost fifty feet into the air. Scientists have been able to date the remains of this central oak very precisely to 95–94 B.C. using tree-ring measurements. Soon after the huge structure was roofed, it was filled with limestone blocks and burned to the ground in what must have been a spectacular bonfire. It's hard to see this enormous hall as anything but a ritual building constructed by a tribal king to celebrate a very special event, perhaps an inauguration or funeral. We can picture hundreds of members of the tribe filing into the structure one night and gaping in awe at the immense hall — and thus the power of the king who built it. After the rituals were completed, the tribe exited and gathered around as the fire was set and consumed the structure. This type of tribal assembly must have been a rare occurrence, but similar events on a lesser scale were crucial parts of the public functions expected of an Irish king.

Kings alone were responsible for dealings with other tribes. In fact, the average member of a tribe, male or female, had no legal rights at all once he or she crossed the tribal boundary. Only the king, his immediate family, and a very restricted class of privileged persons could cross into another tribe's lands. These elite included select tribal leaders, poets, and Druids. Anyone traveling within Ireland, such as Patrick and his companions, would have to have been accompanied by and be under the direct protection of one of these privileged few or he could have been killed with impunity.

Everyone in ancient Ireland had an honor price that an offender would have to pay if that person were injured or insulted. A king was the most valuable, with an honor price of almost thirty cows. A poor, young freeman living with his family rated only a year-old heifer. If someone dared to harm, steal from, dishonor, abuse, or even make fun of a king in a satirical poem, he and his family would likely lose every head of cattle they owned and be reduced to utter poverty.

Irish kings were expected to be dispensers of balanced and fair justice. Woe be to the king who made an unjust judgment. If such a thing happened, stories say that women and cattle would be infertile, crops would fail, and plagues would ravage the tribal lands. A king also had to be brave in battle and perfect of body. If he ran away in a war or was disfigured in some way, he would lose his kingship.

Every king also had a number of taboos placed on him, probably to set him apart from the common people. These peculiar restrictions ranged from the pleasant, such as never passing an alehouse without stopping in, and the inconvenient, such as never sleeping past sunrise, to the bizarre, such as never allowing three red-haired men to go before him into a house.

Kingship was not strictly passed from father to son; a king could be selected from any member of a royal family. Candidates had to pass tests of physical strength and endurance designed to assure the tribe they would be able leaders in war. The finalist was then chosen in a supernatural ceremony called the "bull-sleep." In this ritual a trusted man was selected to eat the meat and drink the broth of a slaughtered bull. While he then slept, four Druids chanted an incantation above him so that he would see in his dreams a vision of the one man destined to be king. If the dreamer was later discovered to have lied, he was killed.

The actual process of inaugurating an Irish king could be quite a shock to a foreigner. In the twelfth century, a Welsh clergyman named Gerald, visiting a remote region of Donegal in western Ireland, came across a ceremony that clearly disgusted him. He says that all the members of a tribe had gathered together one day to confirm their new king. A white female horse was led into the crowd — white always having been a supernatural color among the Celts. The royal candidate then had sexual intercourse with the horse in full view of the people while proclaiming that he too was a beast. The horse was then immediately killed, cut into pieces, and cooked in a giant vat of water. The new king promptly climbed into the pot and drank the broth by dipping in his face while the tribe surrounding him happily feasted on the meat. As strange as this inauguration might have seemed to Gerald and to us, it fits nicely into Celtic mythology. A king was the link between his people and the divinely given lands of the tribe. Because the land was always seen as feminine and often represented as a goddess, the king was joined in a symbolic marriage to the goddess of the land. White horses were supernatural animals, so the sexual act between the king and the horse represented a divine union between him and the goddess of the land.

After an Irish king died, he was remembered for generations by his tribe through the songs of poets. Some of these pre-Christian poems survive from Leinster in southeast Ireland. They are short, forceful compositions highlighting the bravery of ancestors in battle, sometimes against supernatural forces, and their prosperous rule over the tribe:

A king has arrived at the land of the dead,
the glorious son of Sétnae
destroyed the valleys of the Fomorians
under the lands of men.
From the lofty heights of Ailenn,
the mighty leader of many lands
Mess-Telmann of the Fir Domnann
killed the great ones of the earth.

These ancient poems often compare kings to fierce animals:

Bresal Bélach, a giant bear,
a mighty champion, conquered his enemies.
A glorious hero, a fierce warrior,
he destroyed the armies of the sons of Conn.

Sometimes the songs have a distinctly un-Christian tone, betraying their early origins:

Brighter than the great golden sun,
he defeated the lands of men —

Moén, the only son of King Aine,
like a god among the gods.

Patrick must have often heard such verses as he called on tribal leaders, who were always eager to impress visitors with their glorious lineage. A bard would rise by the hearth fire after the evening feast, take his harp in hand, and sing such songs well into the night. Patrick, savvy as he was, would always have been suitably impressed.

The warriors whom the king led were, in the eyes of Patrick and any other civilized Roman, a ragtag assortment of raucous, undisciplined, uncontrollable louts who would melt before a proper Roman legion like butter on a hot day. But they were unfailingly brave. The Greek historian Polybius tells of Celtic warriors in a second-century B.C. account that could just as easily have described Irish fighters of Patrick's time:

> The Celts were all young, powerfully built men with gold torques on their necks and gleaming bands on their arms . . . though they were being slaughtered, they held their ground, equal to the Romans in courage, but inferior in weapons.

In the mind of an ancient Gaul or Irishman, the strategy of fighting an enemy was the same — each man picked an opponent across the lines and hacked at him until one of them fell. There was no grand battle plan or Roman-style coordination with fellow tribe members, just one-on-one combat for honor and glory until the losing side withdrew. And just like their Gaulish cousins, Irish warriors liked to cut off the heads of their defeated enemies and hang them up as trophies in their homes.

Irish warriors of Patrick's time were fearsome opponents on the battlefield. Some stood as tall as six feet, sporting long hair and clean-shaven faces, aside from the bushy, drooping mustaches useful for straining ale at a feast. Each would have been equipped with an impressive array of weapons for battle. Like most Celts, they wore woolen pants, as opposed to the kilt-like uniform of the Roman legionnaire. A tunic reached down below the waist and was brightly colored, with a striped or checkered pattern in glorious reds, blues, and greens. Around the waist was a leather belt holding a razor-sharp sword perhaps three feet in length. Each warrior also carried a wooden shield with a central metal boss — again decorated with richly colored designs. Some wore conical helmets, and all carried lengthy spears with broad points made to tear through an opponent's flesh with ease.

A wonderful early story tells of Irish warriors boasting of their recent kills to earn the honor of the finest slice of pork at a banquet. The Ulsterman Conall brags to his rival Cet from Connacht in the west that

> since I first took up a spear in my hand, not a day has passed that I haven't killed a Connacht warrior, not a night has passed that I haven't burned your lands with fire and slept with a Connacht head under my knee!

Cet reluctantly agrees that Conall is the better man but says that his fellow Connacht warrior Anlúan would teach the Ulsterman a lesson if only he were also at the dinner:

> Oh, but he is, replied Conall, who then reached in his bag and pulled out Anlúan's head, throwing the gory mass onto Cet's lap so that he was covered in blood.

Such tales may not perfectly reflect reality in

ancient Ireland, but they show the spirit and bravado of Irish warriors. Anyone who would be an Irish king had to be able to manage such men.

Medieval stories say that the first king Patrick met was Loíguire, who ruled at Tara as lord of all Irish sovereigns. High King Loíguire was surrounded by Druids who had repeatedly warned him of Patrick's coming. They told of the Christian priest and his mission years before he ever arrived in Ireland:

> *With a head like an adze and a curved*
> * stick he will come,*
> *Chanting his evil songs in his house with*
> * a hole,*
> *From the table in the front of the house,*
> *And his people will say, "So be it, so be it."*

With his head shaved on top — in the Roman fashion — with his bishop's staff of office, chanting the service from the altar in the front of the church, the congregation responding, "amen, amen" — this man was bringing a dangerous new way of life to Ireland, warned Loíguire's Druids. Kill him, they said. Don't listen to his words. He will overthrow kingdoms, destroy our gods, and

146

rule in your place. The stories say that Patrick dared to light a bonfire on the night of Easter, when all fires but the king's were forbidden. Put it out, the Druids cried, or his light will shine ever brighter until you are consumed. Loíguire tried to kill Patrick by poison and magic, but the miracle-working saint slew the Druids, and the king, shaken in his heart, begged Patrick to lead him into the new faith.

The real story of Patrick's dealings with the kings of Ireland is very different. First, there was no high king of Ireland at Tara — the idea of a universal king is a later invention. Second, the story of Patrick, Loíguire, and the Druids owes more to miracle stories from the Old Testament than to memories of actual events. Moses and Aaron battled the magicians of Pharaoh, Elijah contested with the prophets of Baal on Mount Carmel, and the companions of Daniel survived the fiery furnace as a testimony to God. Patrick, in the eyes of his medieval biographers, must have conquered the pagan forces of Ireland in a similar fashion.

However, in reality, Patrick's mission probably succeeded because of a slow and steady approach with a careful eye to the practical politics of Irish society. More than anything else, he needed cooperation from the kings of northern Ireland if he was to minister to the Christians already there and preach the gospel to possible converts. We know from his letters that Patrick made payments to the local kings in order to gain their favor and protection. He was still doing this at the end of his life, so it's reasonable to assume that he was making these payments, probably even more of them, at the beginning of his ministry.

Patrick's mission to Ireland probably began something like this: The leaders of the British church had known of Christian slaves and converts on the northern reaches of the Irish coast for many years, but they never had the manpower to send a permanent mission to these isolated souls. Occasional deacons and priests may have visited the Boyne Valley and surrounding areas during the years before Patrick, but the antagonism of the local Irish kings and the scattered locations of the Christians would have made any consistent work difficult. At some time in the 430s, Patrick persuaded the church leadership to allow him to go to northern Ireland as a minister to the Christians living there. He must have argued that he had the knowledge of Irish culture and language to make the mission work. There undoubtedly was some grumbling that this young man who could barely write a proper Latin sentence was a poor choice for such an important task, but he seemed capable to most of the churchmen, and besides, there wasn't anyone else eager for the job.

Patrick probably began at one of the trading posts on the northeast coast — sites under the protection of a local king and accustomed to visiting Romans with their peculiar Christian ways. There would probably have been a small Christian community already established in the area, centered on the tribal headquarters. Patrick would have first visited the local king and sought his permission to work with the Christians within the tribal borders — a request accompanied by generous gifts of silver and gold and promises of more to come. A small church may have been in use, but much of Patrick's work would have been done at the individual farmsteads. He would have begun by visiting any free Christians in the area, asking about their needs and offering whatever help and guidance he could. Christian slaves in these households would have been especially glad to see a priest, and many from Britain must have been thrilled to hear news from home. Patrick must have done what he could for Christian slaves in pagan households, but he would have had to be careful not to offend their masters and risk bringing down punishment on these slaves. He would have slowly built up his base of supporters among the tribe, discussing the new religion with any curious listeners but not antagonizing the established hierarchy or annoying the local Druids by aggressively proselytizing.

In time Patrick must have sought the assistance of the local king in visiting Christians beyond the tribal borders. In fact, he recruited the sons of kings to accompany him on his journeys. Using such escorts was, however, a tricky business. Young, hotheaded Celtic warriors do not make the best traveling companions, and we know that on at least one occasion the escorts turned from protectors to plunderers, stealing from and threatening Patrick and his men. But as Patrick says, he also had allies among the Irish nobility who rescued him after one such attack.

Patrick used the kings of Ireland for his own purposes, as they used him to gain wealth and perhaps the prestige of having a civilized Roman living and working among them. Some kings must have become Christians over time, which would have made Patrick's work immeasurably easier, though perhaps not less costly. So in this piecemeal fashion, moving from king to king, he slowly but surely spread his ministry to dozens of tribes through the north of Ireland.

Eight

Druids

How wonderful it is that here in Ireland a people who never had any knowledge of God — who until now have worshiped idols and impure things — have recently become a people of the Lord and are now called children of God.

The stories of Patrick's battles with the Druids of King Loíguire are fiction, but they raise the serious question of what sort of religious opposition he faced in Ireland. He probably concentrated on ministering just to Christians at first, but there would have come a time when his success at converting the pagan Irish ran headlong into conflict with native Irish religion. We can hope that it was a peaceful struggle, an enlightened exchange of views between Patrick and followers of Celtic beliefs, but such is rarely the case with religious differences. Patrick would have been a serious threat to whatever religious institutions existed in early Ireland.

Their leaders might at first have dismissed him as just some crazy Roman working with fellow Britons and a few gullible Irish, but when Patrick began to convert the sons and daughters of Irish kings, the native priests were bound to take notice. Some of the violence that he says he faced may not have been based on a simple desire to rob or enslave him but could have been brought about by native priests who wanted to destroy a new religion that they saw spreading like a plague across the tribes.

To understand the sort of religious opposition Patrick may have faced, we have to look at early Celtic and Irish religion. Was there only one religion in the Celtic world? Was it run exclusively by the Druids? How many gods existed in early Irish belief? Did people believe in life after death? If so, what did they imagine such life was like? To answer these questions we have to explore the written evidence on Celtic religion from Greek and Roman authors, look at archaeological finds from Spain to modern Turkey, and examine medieval Welsh and Irish tales that look back at their own early religious history. Each type of evidence is woefully incomplete and must be used with great caution, but with care we can begin to piece together the spiritual environment that Patrick probably encountered in fifth-century Ireland.

The gods of the ancient Celts are similar in many ways to those found in early Greece, Rome, India, or anywhere else polytheism prevailed and numerous gods with various functions existed side by side. In Greece, Zeus was the king of the gods. He tried to control a constantly quarreling and treacherous family of divinities, each jealously guarding his or her allotted corner of the cosmos. Romans had Jupiter to rule over Minerva, Mercury, Juno, Mars, and many others. Ancient Celtic religion, as far as we can tell, also had a number of gods and goddesses responsible for various functions, but we run into serious trouble when we try to understand these divine powers. To begin with, almost everything we know about early Celtic religion comes to us by way of the Greeks and Romans, who were often prejudiced against their subjects. Those few classical writers who treat Celtic religion in a positive light suffer from a surplus of idealism and a desire to turn the Celts into noble savages uncorrupted by the perceived vices of Mediterranean society. The Greeks and

Romans also tended to focus on the Druids to the exclusion of other forms of religion — probably because druidic teachings seemed so exotic and barbaric to the classical world. This tendency leaves us with a sketchy picture of daily religious life among the ancient Celts, but what we can piece together about Celtic religion in the days before Christianity gives us an intriguing glimpse into a world vastly different from our own.

The one god who appears time and again all over the ancient Celtic world — from Roman Spain and Gaul to medieval Wales and Ireland — is Lugus, literally "the shining one." Julius Caesar ran across images of Lugus throughout Gaul during his conquest and described the god as similar to the Roman Mercury. Caesar says Lugus was the inventor of all arts and a guide on every journey. This may not sound like the most exciting role for a major god, but it's likely that there was much more to the worship of Lugus than Caesar records. His importance is shown by the number of towns throughout Europe that bear variants of his name, such as Lyons in France, Leiden in Holland, and Lugudunum (the fort of Lugus) in Roman Britain. Lugus also shows up on an early inscription from Spain celebrating a religious festival, and in the great Irish feast of Lughnasadh on August 1. In medieval Wales he was Lleu, the magical shoemaker.

As the god Lug in early Ireland, he was called "skilled at many arts" and was a handsome young divinity who in one telling story arrived late for a feast. The gatekeeper asked who he was and what skill he possessed that the court might use. While running through a list of his abilities, from writing poetry to forging iron and inventing board games, Lug was repeatedly rebuffed by the guard, who said they already had someone who could do such things. "Yes," Lug responded, "but do you have someone who can do everything?" He was then allowed into the feast. A god who could fashion anything was a powerful deity to the Celts, who were known far and wide for their craftsmanship, often exceeding even that of the civilized Greeks and Romans.

No other god is found as widely in Celtic lands as Lugus, but we do know of a few regional and local divinities. Belenus, known from Gaul, northern Italy, and Britain, seems to have been a healing god connected with the sun, like Greek Apollo. The mother goddess Matrona and her divine son, Maponus, occur in Gaul and Britain, while the goddess Brigantia (the exalted one) is found in northern Celtic lands. Brigantia's cult survived the coming of Christianity by transferring aspects of her worship to her Irish namesake, St. Brigid, whose feast day falls on the important pre-Christian spring festival of Imbolg. The Celtic goddess Epona was especially associated with horses, and her cult was adopted by the Roman cavalry. In Welsh tales she survives as the powerful and wise queen Rhiannon, while in Irish stories the swift-footed Macha is a goddess closely connected with horses. Numerous other gods occur in Gaul who seem to have been present in Ireland as well, such as Cernunnos, a horned god of animals, Dis Pater, the dark god of the dead, and Ogmios, a Hercules-like divine champion. The Latin poet Lucan describes three additional gods from Gaul:

Cruel Teutates happy with bloody sacrifices,
Horrible Esus with his barbarous altars,
and Taranis, with worship more fearful than
 Scythian Diana.

Later writers say that victims of Teutates were drowned in caldrons, while those of

Esus and Taranis were hung from trees and burned in wooden cages.

Women had a crucial role in Celtic religion, as far as we can determine from ancient reports. One early story tells of a cult of women on an island off Gaul who performed a chilling annual ritual. Every year they would tear the roof off their temple and feverishly rebuild it during a single day. Each woman would carry a load of roofing material to the temple. On a prearranged signal, one of the women would be bumped and drop her load, at which point the rest would tear her into pieces while shouting ecstatically to their god. Other evidence is more benign and comes from the Celtic women themselves. A first-century A.D. lead tablet from southern Gaul lists the names of another cultic group of women who called themselves *mnas brictom* (women of magic) and wove spells and predicted the future.

Many of the descriptions of the Druids in ancient Gaul derive from a Greek philosopher named Posidonius, who lived in the first century B.C. As a young man, Posidonius traveled among the Gauls before they were conquered by the Romans. Thus, while we shouldn't take everything he says at face value, his testimony is generally trustworthy. Posidonius says that Gaulish Druids studied the ways of nature, supervised sacred rites, presided over public and private disputes, and were able to stop wars simply by stepping between opposing armies. They and their assistants would predict the future by stabbing a sacrificial victim, often a criminal, in the stomach and watching how his blood spurted from the wound or how he convulsed on the ground while dying.

The most important teaching of the Druids was that life is eternal. Contrary to the Greek and Roman teachings of a pallid, dreary afterlife in the land of Hades, the Druids believed that human spirits are reincarnated, with the soul passing into a new body after a number of years. Some Celts would even agree to put off repaying a debt until their next life. The Romans said this belief was cynical propaganda designed to make Gaulish warriors less fearful of death in battle, but many cultures in ancient times shared similar beliefs. Caesar adds that the Druids were an elite group who underwent up to twenty years of training. The length of study was necessary because no teaching of the Druids was ever written down — every

159

scrap of knowledge was preserved in verse and had to be memorized.

Of the few individual Druids we know from classical sources, most were actually women. Druidism was apparently an equal opportunity priesthood, though we can't be sure women were able to hold all offices and perform every duty. It may be that Druids existed in parallel groups of men and women, such as many modern religious orders do, or that women were allotted special roles, such as prophecy and healing. The few druidic rites we know of, besides human sacrifice, involve medical treatment with mistletoe and marsh grasses, the creation of good-luck amulets, or fortune-telling, specifically by female Druids. But women in the druidic religious order could be quite fearsome. Tacitus describes some of these Druids during the Roman invasion of the Welsh island of Anglesey in A.D. 60:

> The shore of the island was crowded with the mass of the enemy. All around their soldiers were women with wild hair like Furies waving sticks at our troops. The Druids were all crying to their gods and calling down curses on us — a sight which terrified the Roman soldiers.

Tacitus says that after all the Druids were killed, the Romans destroyed their sacred groves and altars covered with human blood and entrails.

Many modern readers of classical descriptions of bloody human sacrifice by the Druids have been understandably skeptical. They ask how a religious priesthood supposedly based on understanding and applying the great rhythmical and cyclical teachings of the universe could practice such gruesome rituals. Surely, they say, this must be a deliberate misrepresentation by the Romans designed to justify their conquests and oppression of the Celts. The problem with such an interpretation is that we cannot impose our own values on the Druids. Plenty of societies, both ancient and modern, have had no trouble mixing blood and philosophy. The Romans themselves had a history of human sacrifice in religious ceremonies as late as the Punic Wars against Hannibal. Another problem with modern skepticism concerning the Druids is archaeological evidence. A Celtic temple at Roquepertuse in southern Gaul contains niches for human skulls, while recent excavations elsewhere in Gaul have uncovered what appear to be dedications — the remains of large groups of decapitated warriors. In just the last few years, archaeologists have also found clear evidence of human sacrifice among the Galatian Celts of Asia Minor. Such physical testimony is a powerful argument that the classical authors, while perhaps exaggerating on occasion, were essentially correct in their descriptions of Celtic religious practices.

Even with archaeological confirmation of Celtic human sacrifice, however, we have to be careful not to see such gruesome activities as central to Celtic religion. The average Celt living in pre-Roman Gaul would rarely have witnessed these bloody ceremonies and would have cared much more about honoring his or her local gods with small dedications and perhaps the sacrifice of an occasional goat. Ensuring a good harvest, a daughter's marriage, healthy old age — these were the sorts of religious issues most Celts focused on. A good example of private Celtic religion comes from the source of the Seine River in central France, where countless small wooden images have been uncovered. Here Celtic pilgrims would place in the water a small carved statue of themselves or an ailing body part as a supplication to the goddess Sequana in hope of comfort and healing.

The primary sources for Celtic religion in Ireland are tales dating from medieval Christian times that recall the days before the faith arrived on the island. These sources are a treasure trove of information, but we have to be cautious in our interpretations since they were all recorded by Christian clergy or those trained in a Christian setting.

In the Irish epic *Táin Bó Cuailnge*, for example, the warrior queen Medb and her husband, Ailill, command a massive force that invades the land of Ulster to capture a glorious bull. Medb is the epitome of a fierce and powerful female leader who inspires armies and practices a promiscuity unavailable to the average Irish woman. "I've never been with a man unless I had another waiting in the wings," she boldly tells her husband, from whom she demands a total lack of jealousy in spite of her frequent and open dalliances. Medb, whose name means "intoxicating," has a role that is clearly supernatural and pre-Christian in origin. She offers herself to the best and strongest of warriors and kings as a reward for bravery and loyalty.

Just underneath the medieval story, it's tempting to see Medb as a Celtic sovereignty goddess who dispenses power and legitimizes rule as a representative of the divine land.

Neolithic tombs played a large role in the Irish mythology of Patrick's time and beyond. To enter the great mound of Newgrange, north of Dublin, is to sense something of the awe these monuments inspired. Although the passage into Newgrange itself was blocked until modern times, many such mounds throughout Ireland were open to anyone brave enough to enter. Newgrange stands more than two hundred feet in diameter and rises high above the surrounding countryside. It was built with enormous amounts of labor and required considerable architectural skill. In front of the single entrance on the southeast face is a huge stone carved with intricate spirals. Climb around this barrier, and you will see above the portal a small, boxlike opening designed to allow light into the narrow passageway leading to the heart of the mound. Carefully work your way deeper inside the tomb, and you will emerge into a room diverging into three recessed chambers, each holding a repository for the bones of long-dead ancestors. For those who don't mind the thought of tons of earth over their heads, a miraculous sight occurs on the winter solstice. At sunrise a narrow beam of light penetrates the perfectly aligned opening above the entrance and briefly shines through eighty feet of darkness to strike the rear wall of the burial chamber.

These burial mounds played a part in an important idea in pre-Christian Irish religion — the concept of the Otherworld. The tombs were believed to be entrances to a realm that was sometimes a land of the dead and sometimes a land of supernatural forces parallel to our own world. The barrier between the two domains was normally fixed, but at times such as the festival of Samain [Halloween], the veil separating the realms could fall. In one early Irish tale, Medb and Ailill were huddled with their tribe in their feast hall on Samain night, fearful of spirits and gods roaming the land. They offered a reward to anyone who would dare to go outside and tie a twig around the foot of a dead man hanging from the gallows. All the warriors shrank in fear, but a young man named Nera volunteered to go forth. Just as Nera finished the task, the dead man nonchalantly asked him for a drink of water, which Nera gladly gave him. Then on the way back to Medb and Ailill, Nera saw the hall of his king and queen burning and a troop of Otherworld warriors marching away. He followed them into a hole in the ground where it was spring, the opposite of time in his own world. After a series of strange encounters, which included getting a fairy woman pregnant, he left the cave, only to discover that he had been living in the future and still had a chance to save his tribe in this world. Otherworld stories often involve such shifting of time and space, in the mode more of modern science fiction than of standard medieval tales. The Otherworld could be underground; it could also be on a faraway island or even a part of our everyday world, but only for those who could see it.

The Celtic idea of rebirth also appears in early Irish literature. A good example is a story in which a Christian missionary discovered an aged monk named Tuán, who had lived in Ireland since the arrival of the first inhabitants. He had grown old as the last survivor of the first settlers, fleeing from wolves and living in caves until at last one night he changed into a deer. After that life was over, he became a boar, then a hawk, and finally a salmon. One day he was caught and eaten by a woman in whose womb he began to grow. He was born again as a human baby and lived many years until he met Patrick and was baptized as a Christian.

In early Irish stories, Druids serve as priests, counselors, and teachers, as well as prophets. One tale records that the Druid Cathbad was passing by a royal enclosure one day when a young woman asked him what the present hour was good for. He responded that whoever conceived a child at that time would bear a king. Since Cathbad was the only man around, the woman grabbed him to make love with her.

During the early days of Christianity in Ireland, Druids still maintained many of their ancient rights and powers. Treaties were sworn in their presence, and their curses were greatly feared. In one particularly powerful and lethal spell, a Druid would stand on one leg with one arm raised and one eye closed in imitation of a crane. Irish Druids could also reportedly guarantee victory in battle or kill warriors who defied their power.

But the Druids of early Ireland slowly

lost their prestige as Christianity spread. Law texts several centuries after Patrick treat the surviving members of the order more as pathetic sorcerers than as powerful priests. They were still feared in later times for their curses, but they were no longer honored. Many seem to have barely eked out a living by concocting love potions in huts hidden away in the forest.

Medieval Irish sources speak of Druids living in Ireland during ancient times, but we also hear of wonder-working poets who appear to have taken over many druidic powers after Christianity arrived. He or she — we have several references to female poets — was first of all a respected professional who could have an honor price as high as that of a king. Such a bard could raise a ruler to prominence through songs or destroy a person through satire. Poets had many magical powers, including predicting the future. When Medb meets the female poet Fedelm in the *Táin*, the queen asks what will be the fate of her army in the upcoming battle. "I see crimson, I see red" is the answer Fedelm gives her. There were set rituals to gain such knowledge that survived the arrival of Christianity, but these rituals faced constant disapproval from the church. In the *imbas forosnai* ceremony, for example, the Irish poet first had to find a suitable dog to eat. Dogs were valuable as household guardians and for hunting, so few people were willing to give theirs up, but the poet could also use a pig or a cat. If a bard could find an animal, he would chew on its raw flesh until it was softened, then place it on a stone behind the door of his darkened hut. Finally, with prayers said, he would lie immobile for one, two, or even three days until he received a vision from the gods.

The religious world that Patrick encountered in Ireland was challenging to say the least. A potential Irish convert would have grown up in a land with many gods, a land with Druids and magical bards, a land where the mysterious, invisible Otherworld was always present and watching. Patrick faced enormous difficulties in convincing the Irish that his imported religion better reflected the truth of the universe than the teachings they had received from their ancestors. What he did have going for him was a passionate conviction that he was right. He also offered a new way, a new model of life for anyone tired of the constraints of Irish society and religion. As early Christianity appealed especially to slaves and women in the Roman Empire, Patrick's faith found its warmest reception in Ireland among those on the fringes of society.

Nine

Virgins

You can see that the sons and daughters of Irish kings have become brothers and virgins for Christ. One of these Irish women was of noble birth — full grown and quite beautiful really — whom I had baptized.

The life of a woman in early Ireland was not easy. Modern stories sometimes suggest that, before Patrick, Ireland enjoyed a kind of golden age of Celtic paganism, which included equality between the sexes — but there is simply no evidence for this claim in historical sources. However, the lot of an Irish woman was not necessarily so bad compared with those of her counterparts in ancient Greece and Rome. In Ireland women had a few rights and privileges that even a Roman matron might have envied. Still, early Ireland was a land run primarily by and for men. Into this world stepped Patrick, who brought with him Christian ideas of equality between the sexes, at least in the world to come. Moreover, Christianity taught that in this life there is a basic human dignity to be granted to everyone. This surely is one reason why Patrick's message had such an appeal to the women of Ireland. Time and again in his letters he writes of his many female followers and his deep concern for them. They came from all ranks of society, from the daughters of kings to the lowest slave women. Free and slave, native or foreign-born, they were to Patrick the heart and soul of his mission. But what was life like for a woman in Patrick's Ireland?

Irish law texts tell us that women were classed along with children, slaves, and insane persons as having no independent legal rights. This doesn't mean that they could be abused at will, but their legal protections were based on their relationship to whichever man had authority over them, be it father, husband, or son. This was true in many early societies. A Roman woman also passed seamlessly from the care of her father to her husband and, if she was widowed, to her son or other male family member. All Roman women, such as those in Patrick's childhood home, were under the guardianship of a male. One of the earliest Roman laws states plainly the rule that governed women for centuries: "Women, even if they are full grown, shall always have a legal guardian because of their foolish minds."

We can enjoy stories of Medb leading armies in the *Táin*, but we hear nothing of historic Irish women leading warriors or ruling kingdoms. In ancient Gaul, Celtic women would supposedly join their husbands in war if the tide turned against their men, and perhaps this happened on occasion in Ireland as well, but the admirable qualities of a woman recorded in early Irish texts do not include the ability to decapitate an enemy on the battlefield. Modesty, virtue, and steady, hard work were the marks of a proper wife. Sexual promiscuity and dabbling in witchcraft were the qualities a man should beware of when shopping for a mate.

Almost all the references we possess to women in early Irish laws are related to marriage. But marriage in ancient Ireland was not as simple as it is today. There were, in fact, at least nine types of marriage in which an Irish man and woman might be bound. In the first and highest form, a man and a woman both contributed goods, such as cattle, and the woman was known as a "wife of joint authority." The second type of marriage was between a man of means and a woman who brought little or nothing to the union. In the third form, a man contributed few if any goods to a prosperous wife. The fourth category of marriage occurred when a man spent the night with a woman occasionally at her home, always with her family's consent. The fifth type was when a woman willfully eloped with a man without her father's approval. In the sixth form of marriage, a woman reluctantly allowed herself to be abducted from her home without her family's knowledge. In the seventh form, a man visited a woman secretly in her home without her father's consent. The eighth type of union was with a mentally incompetent spouse, in which case Irish law acted vigorously to protect the person of unsound mind from exploitation. The final type of sexual union was not a consensual bond but an act of rape. In such a case it made no legal difference if the man or woman was drunk or incapacitated — the man paid a heavy fine plus the cost of raising any children resulting from the act. Indeed, in almost all cases the man bore full financial responsibility for a child resulting from even the most random sexual encounter.

Raising children in early Ireland often involved a custom that may seem very odd to modern parents — placing children in the long-term care of foster parents. Unlike our society, in which foster care is usually a situation of last resort resulting from the death or inability of a mother or father to provide for a child, Irish fosterage in the time of Patrick and well into the Middle Ages was a common and sought-after arrangement. Both boys and girls were sent out to foster parents from an early age, even as babies, by prosperous families as means of building alliances between kin groups. Sometimes the foster parents were paid a fee to take on a child, but families were often eager to accept children from the outside — especially if an alliance with those children's families might prove useful. This doesn't mean, though, that fosterage was a purely business relationship. In fact, the Old Irish affectionate terms for parents equivalent to our "mommy" and "daddy" were given to the foster parents, not the birth parents.

Foster parents taught children from beyond their kin group all the necessary skills of life and provided them with a loving home environment just as they did for their own sons and daughters. Foster children knew and visited their natural parents, but the closest parental relationship they experienced was with the family who raised them day by day. Fosterage often lasted late into the teenage years, when a foster father would present the child with a parting gift. One can imagine that the end of fosterage was an emotional scene, as the child, now an adult, returned to live permanently with his or her birth family. But strong links remained between foster families and children long into adulthood. In times of trouble, foster families and their former charges would rise to aid, protect, or avenge each other as they would their closest relatives. Irish stories even speak of foster brothers embracing in the heat of battle though they might be on opposite sides.

Polygamy was probably common in Ireland through the Middle Ages, though the church tried its best to discourage the practice. A man could marry one woman in a high form of marriage while joining with another in a lower form. If the man brought home a second wife, she was under the supervision of his chief spouse — who was incidentally allowed to beat the second wife for the first three days. In reality, many senior wives probably welcomed the additional help on the farm.

A woman's life in early Ireland, like a man's, revolved around agriculture. Most tasks on the farm could be done by either men or women, but certain chores seem to have habitually fallen to the wife or wives. A man sheared the sheep, but the woman turned it into wool and wove clothing for her family. Women were usually responsible for milking the cows, making butter and cheese, and fattening up pigs for slaughter. And as in most societies, it was the woman who cooked the meals and raised the children. A woman with no brothers could legally inherit and run the family farm. If such a woman later married a man with no property or a husband from another tribe, she retained control of all financial and legal matters.

If a woman's lot became too hard, divorce was an option. A woman who simply grew tired of her husband and abandoned him lost all rights to marital property and community respect. But there were numerous recognized and acceptable reasons for a woman to end a marriage. If a man left his wife for another woman, she could divorce him and, along with her share of the household property, go back to her father. If a man spread vicious rumors about his wife or composed a satire against her, she could sue for divorce. If he told intimate details of their relationship openly without her permission, she could leave him. If a husband ever struck his wife so that he caused a bruise or blemish on her, she could divorce him without contest. Irish husbands also had certain sexual obligations. If a man became impotent or grew too fat for sexual intercourse, a wife could freely leave him. If a woman wanted to have children and her husband could not fulfill his marital duties, she could remain married to him but legally seek out another man to get her pregnant. Her husband was obliged to treat any child resulting from such a union as his own.

When Patrick began to convert the daughters of Ireland, especially those of the nobility, to Christianity, he ran headlong into Irish customs and tradition. An Irish maiden — and she had to be a virgin for a proper marriage — was a most valuable asset to any father wishing to improve his lot in life. The strategic marriage of a king's daughter could even settle border disputes, increase a tribe's land, or end years of bloody hostility.

One of the most engaging passages in Patrick's letters tells of such a daughter:

One of these Irish women was of noble birth — full grown and quite beautiful really — whom I had baptized. A few days after this, she came to me with something important on her mind. She said that an angel from God had appeared to her and told her she should become a virgin of Christ if she wanted to be closer to God. Thanks be to God — six days later she joyfully and wholeheartedly chose that path which all virgins of God take.

We can imagine the reaction of this young woman's father, even if he was a Christian himself, to her announcement that she was dedicating body as well as soul to God. He probably had arranged a good marriage for her years earlier with a young man of equal rank. And we shouldn't think that Irish fathers were purely selfish in managing their daughters' marriage plans. Any decent and loving father would want to see his daughter joined with a man who would provide for her needs and protect her when he would no longer be alive to care for her. A daughter who chose this new form of perpetual virginity was essentially opting out of the entire social system. If a girl ran off with some stranger, she would at least be protected under Irish law as a partner in a low but recognized form of marriage. But to promise her virginity to an invisible God left her in a situation that must have deeply worried any Irish father or mother. Patrick himself describes the frequently negative reaction experienced by women who chose the chaste path:

> Many of them do this against the wishes of their parents. Indeed, their families sometimes punish them cruelly and make all sorts of horrible accusations against them.

Some young women who decided to devote their bodies to God likely changed their minds after a few weeks of such overwhelming family pressure. But many stuck with it. As Patrick says:

> The number of such virgins who have chosen this new life continues to grow

so that I can't keep track of them all.

Spiritual benefits aside, a life of Christian chastity gave women a choice that had never been possible before — they could gain some control over their lives and bodies. Before Patrick, marriage and children were the only option available to them. Now a whole new way of life was possible for those who wanted it badly enough to risk estrangement from their families.

Sexual continence was not just for Irish virgins. Patrick says that the growing number of those choosing celibacy included widows and even married women. These women also stood to gain control over their lives. Widows could escape being married off by a male relative anxious to rid himself of an unwanted burden. For married women, celibacy was perhaps the best of both worlds. They retained all the honor, property, and privileges of a wife but could end the cycle that left them perpetually pregnant. None of this is to say that Irish women choosing chastity weren't sincerely seeking spiritual grace, just that there were practical benefits to such a choice.

Of the women of Ireland who chose a

life of celibacy, Patrick felt most deeply for the female slaves:

> Sadly, of such women, the ones who suffer the most are the slaves. They face rape and constant threats but suffer this abuse bravely. God gives these women the grace to follow courageously in his path even though they are forbidden to do so.

These slaves would have included women captured abroad as well as native Irish converts. Irish daughters, widows, and wives may have faced a difficult road in choosing chastity, but they at least had legal rights and social customs that guarded them from abuse. Slave women were mere pieces of property, who enjoyed no such protections. Many female slaves routinely suffered sexual abuse from their masters, who had no interest in declarations of celibacy they may have made to the Christian God. But to the best of their ability, these women tried to uphold the ideals of chastity as taught by Patrick.

The idea of religious celibacy in the ancient world dates to long before the rise of Christianity. Priests and priestesses from any number of cults in the Mediterranean world practiced abstinence as a form of devotion to their divinities and as a means of avoiding the entanglements of marriage and family life. Celibacy arose late in Jewish religion but was restricted to a few groups, such as the Essenes in the Judaean wilderness.

Jesus is never described in the New Testament as being married, an unusual situation for a Jewish man, which has led some to speculate that he was an Essene himself. The apostle Paul emphasized Christian abstinence as an ideal but optional way of life in his letters. Throughout the early days of Christianity, both men and women regularly forswore sexual intercourse to draw closer to God. Most of the celibates in the first four centuries of Christianity lived in their family homes or at the edges of villages. They were for the most part highly regarded by fellow Christians, but some did develop a holier-than-thou attitude, which the Church Fathers condemned. In general, though, early Christian leaders praised celibacy, and many practiced it themselves. These Christians did not condemn marriage, but they often saw it as a necessary evil for the production of children. Some Christian couples would live together in a state of abstinence after the birth of a child or two, having fulfilled the divine command to go forth and multiply. There were from an early date houses of Christian virgins, in which women young and old could come together in communities of mutual support and protection. Sometimes unrelated celibate men and women would live in so-called spiritual marriages, but this practice was condemned by Christian teachers as an invitation to sin.

The deserts of Egypt had always attracted a few particularly devoted Christian ascetics. In the fourth century, a young man named Anthony heard the gospel reading telling him to sell all he had and give it to the poor in order to be perfect. He decided to take the command literally and headed out into the desert across the Nile. For twenty years he lived a solitary life, until his reputation for holiness spread and he began to attract the crowds he had tried so hard to avoid. He moved deeper into the desert, but his admirers always found him. Eventually he gave up the fight for solitude and instead organized the followers into communities of loosely associated monks. From these humble beginnings, monastic communities spread like wildfire through the Christian East. In the early days of their religion, martyrdom had been the ultimate sacrifice for Christians. But with Constantine's conversion and the end of persecutions, the ascetic life became a kind of substitute martyrdom, a living sacrifice of one's life and body to God.

St. Jerome was an early proponent of monasticism among Christian men and women, but it was the converted pagan and former Roman soldier Martin who established the monastic way of life in the west of the Empire in the 360s. He founded monasteries in Gaul and was even elected bishop of Tours, though he never let his ecclesiastical office interfere with his life as a celibate monk. Monasteries spread rapidly through Gaul, perhaps even to Britain, in the years just before Patrick's birth.

Patrick may have been trained as a monk himself, but the only evidence we have is his own letters, which, as is often the case, leave us with more questions than answers. Several times in both letters he speaks with enthusiastic approval of those Irish Christians who had chosen a celibate lifestyle, so it's hard to imagine he didn't follow the path himself. He certainly never mentions having a wife, though marriage was still permitted for priests in the Western Church during Patrick's day.

However, advocating and practicing celibacy was not quite the same as being a monk. When we think of monastic life, the picture in our minds is shaped by medieval practices — groups of hooded nuns or monks living together under a strict rule, isolation from the world, a life of prayer and solemn hymns in the early morning hours. But in Patrick's time monasticism was still in its infancy. Many of his Irish followers who chose a celibate life probably continued to live with their families and tribes rather than in separate communities. We can't rule out the existence of monasteries or convents as such in fifth-century Ireland, but we have no evidence for them.

We don't know whether Patrick was a monk or a founder of monasteries, only that he advocated a life of virginity and celibacy for those of his Irish followers, male or female, who aspired to such a calling. He never condemned those who practiced sexual relations within Christian marriage, but for Patrick, as for Paul and Jerome before him, celibacy was the ideal sexual lifestyle for a devout Christian.

Ten

The Ends of the Earth

I can testify that the good news has been preached to the very edge of the inhabited world.

Patrick's relations with kings, Druids, and women in Ireland were powerful external factors in his Christian ministry, but as he traveled and worked throughout the island, one overriding internal force was constantly pushing him — the belief that he was working at the edge of the world and at the end of time. Again and again in both of his letters, Patrick clearly states this idea:

> I am one of those God has called and chosen to preach the good news, even in the most difficult of times, to the very ends of the earth.

This was not some colorful metaphor but an absolute truth. To Patrick, Christianity had to be preached through the entire world, to its very limits and with the greatest urgency, before the fast-approaching end-time. And what place could lie closer to the end of the earth than Ireland?

The first-century A.D. Greek geographer Strabo said that Ireland was a frozen land at the edge of the earth, but he was echoing an even older tradition. To men such as Plato and Alexander, Caesar and Virgil, the Mediterranean lands were, as the very name means, the center of the world. They knew very well, centuries before Columbus, that the earth was a giant sphere. They would have laughed at any notion of falling off the edge of the world, as would any educated person during the Middle Ages. The boundaries the Greeks and Romans knew were dictated not by the shape of the earth but by its climate. The Mediterranean Sea lay in a temperate zone in which people and animals could prosper. Summers were hot and winters might be cold, but with the shade of an olive tree to keep cool or a warm fire on a wintry night, the weather was quite bearable and pleasant. But disaster and death awaited anyone who strayed beyond the temperate boundaries of the earth. To the south of the Mediterranean world lay the vast Sahara desert of Africa. To the north were the frozen wastelands of northern Europe and Asia. Many serious scholars and most of the general public believed that human life simply wasn't possible in these distant regions. The gods had bound the livable world with ice to the north and fire to the south. Stories circulated occasionally of travelers who had crossed the desert to see jungles and faraway kingdoms in Africa or lived to tell of habitable lands to the far north, but these reports were generally dismissed. Strabo is typical when he says that a Greek named Pytheas, who supposedly sailed to the northern seas around Iceland — the mythical Thule — was "the greatest of liars."

Ancient geographers were willing to concede that there might be another temperate zone in the earth's southern hemisphere, far beyond the burning region of the equator. They even thought these lands might be inhabited and gave the name Antipodes or "upside-down feet" to the people who supposedly lived there. But because of the uncrossable divide of the boiling equatorial regions, those from the Mediterranean world could not visit there any more than they could travel to the moon.

Julius Caesar was the first to call Ireland "Hibernia," a form of the native Irish name, but also Latin for "winterland." Strabo drew on earlier Greek geographers such as Eratosthenes and placed Ireland north of Britain on the edge of the frozen sea. To Strabo and others, Ireland was the last stop in the inhabited world for anyone heading north:

> If you would go north . . . from the center of Britain, you would come to a land which is only barely habitable — this is the region of Ireland. Areas lying farther to the north, such as Thule, cannot support life.

Though Greek and Roman writers later realized that Ireland in fact lay to the west of Britain, many still maintained that it was on the boundary of the habitable world. Others were still unsure about the island's climate. Even in the days of Patrick's childhood, the Latin court poet Claudian called Ireland a frozen land.

Patrick knew better than anyone that Ireland, while sometimes chilly, was not Strabo's frigid island where the wretched inhabitants barely eked out a living among snow and ice. But from his own experience and from his Roman education, Patrick knew that Ireland lay at the extreme northwest boundary of an inhabited world that stretched eastward and southward to Gaul, Italy, Greece, Persia, even to India and the mysterious land of the Seres or "silk people" in the farthest East. Even today, if we stand on the Cliffs of Moher in County Clare or look west over the ocean from the village of Glencolumbkille in County Donegal, we see an endless sea stretching to the setting sun. It is not hard to imagine, as Patrick believed, that the western coast of Ireland is truly the limit of the world. Patrick even modifies a biblical passage in one of his quotations to drive this belief home. In the Gospel of Matthew, Jesus says that in the latter days "many will come from the east and west" to feast with the patriarchs in the kingdom of Heaven. Patrick quite consciously adds "and from the north and south" to emphasize that his converts in Ireland would also share in the everlasting heavenly banquet.

Patrick knew that other ministers had already traveled to the east and south bearing the gospel. Christian churches in the fifth century stretched from Spain and Gaul to India, Ethiopia, and perhaps even China. The one land, in Patrick's worldview, that still remained largely untouched by the Christian message was Ireland.

Besides working at the very ends of the earth, Patrick saw himself laboring in the last days of human history. There was a long tradition, stretching back even before the rise of Christianity, that the end of the world was very close. Jewish culture developed an apocalyptic philosophy and literature in the late centuries B.C. that pervaded Roman Palestine in the time of Jesus. In such beliefs the final act in the great drama of human history was about to come to an abrupt close. God would wash away the sinful world as he did in the days of Noah — but this time with fire — and establish a new order for those who followed his ways. The idea of the fast-approaching last days carried over into the teachings of Jesus and is found throughout the New Testament. The apostle Paul states repeatedly that followers of Christ are living in the last days and that the rule of God on earth is imminent. The entire final book of the New Testament, commonly called Revelation, is known in Greek as the Apocalypse of John and provides an elaborate vision of the coming end of the present age.

The passing away of the first generation of Christians did little to temper these catastrophic beliefs. Second-century Christians produced works such as the Apocalypse of Peter and the Epistle of Barnabas, warning that the end was rapidly approaching. However, as time continued to pass and the world remained intact, some Christian writers began to shift their attention from the coming judgment of God to an emphasis on a more personal and immediate vision of salvation available to all believers in the here and now. From the close of the second century and into the third, there was a marked shift in Christian thought away from the idea that history would soon reach its end. But increased persecution of Christians by Romans in the third century revived the emphasis on an evil world soon to be destroyed in a blaze of fire by the righteous judgment of God.

The fourth and fifth centuries continued the older Christian idea of a world on the brink of destruction. In the view of many theologians in the late Roman Empire, God was about to slam shut the gates of paradise and stoke up the fires of Hell. This shift in attitude is understandable when we consider that barbarians were pouring across the Roman borders and creating havoc throughout the provinces. Rome itself, mother of cities, was sacked — and the Germanic tribes weren't finished. In the minds of many Christians of Patrick's time, these events simply had to signal the end of the world. Rome was falling — how could civilization, how could life, continue? In spite of powerful voices such as that of Augustine, who urged Christians to remain calm and look beyond their world centered on an earthly Rome, many truly believed they were living in the final days of human history.

Patrick clearly shared this view. As he writes to the soldiers of Coroticus:

> I'm not doing all this work for my own satisfaction but for God. He gives me consolation in my heart that I am one of those hunters and fishermen of souls who he says would come in the last days.

And in his *Confession* Patrick declares to the British bishops:

> God heard my prayers so that I, foolish though I am, might dare to undertake such a holy and wonderful mission in

these last days — that I, in my own way, might be like those God said would come to preach and be witness to the good news to all nonbelievers before the end of the world.

We have to put ourselves inside Patrick's mind to see the importance of this idea to his work. Patrick was not a fanatic wandering the streets with a sign warning of the coming destruction of the world. He did not necessarily believe that history would end and the judgment of God would come next week, next year, or even during his lifetime. He in fact worked ceaselessly to lay the foundations for long-term Christian work in Ireland. But to Patrick the time of the world's end was a fixed date that was drawing ever closer. The gospel had been preached throughout the world and was even then, by his own efforts, being spread to the most distant land of all. There was simply no reason for God's judgment to be delayed once the Irish had heard the good news. Patrick would not have presumed to predict a day and time that only God knew, but he saw it as his mission to spread the Christian message to as many Irish souls as possible before it was too late.

Eleven

Coroticus

God . . . what can I do? My flock has
been torn to pieces and scattered by
these wicked men, under the orders of
the evil-minded Coroticus.

Year after year Patrick worked among the
people of Ireland. Children he had baptized
when he arrived became grown men and
women with sons and daughters of their
own. This new generation of Christians sat
at Patrick's feet and heard him tell of Noah
and the ark, David and mighty Goliath, and
Jesus multiplying the loaves and fishes — the
same stories their parents had heard. Patrick's flock grew from just a handful to hundreds, then probably to thousands through
the north of Ireland. He visited tribes and
clans from the Boyne Valley in the east to the
great cliffs overlooking the Western Sea. Not
everyone accepted his message. There were
still plenty of kings, Druids, and common
farmers who wanted nothing to do with this

strange new religion. The old gods had always taken care of them, and they saw no need to listen to this Roman with his talk of brotherhood and stories of a foreign god. Sometimes Patrick could convert a tribal king to Christianity, but these were rare victories. He would at least try to convince the king, often with substantial bribes, to allow a small church to be built on the tribal lands to serve nearby Christians. But for the most part, Patrick worked farm by farm, clan by clan, spreading his message to anyone who would listen.

A typical farmstead would have consisted of an extended family with a few slaves to work in the fields and help with household chores. Patrick would always show the utmost respect for the man of the house, bringing a gift of a British woolen cloak or perhaps a jar of wine from Gaul. But it was the women Patrick concentrated on. If he could win them over, the men would inevitably follow. If a household believed in his teachings and decided to convert, Patrick would return several times to instruct them in the faith. Sometimes, as he grew older, he would send one of the native Irish priests he had ordained to complete the necessary training. On Easter morning the clan would gather at its home or at the local church to receive baptism.

The baptism of the converts began when Patrick's assistant took a small caldron and began heating the water. When all was ready, the men and women disrobed and handed their clothes to waiting attendants. Some modern readers might be shocked that Patrick baptized adults in the nude, but this was a common practice and a tradition going back to the earliest days of Christianity — when a convert was born into a new life, it seemed fitting that he or she should be naked as a baby. A wonderful illustration of early baptism comes from a lead tank found at Walesby in Britain. On the panel is a naked woman flanked by two female attendants, with six males standing near as witnesses. Like the woman portrayed in the British scene, Patrick's converts would first face west to renounce the devil, then turn east to recite the creed and affirm their faith. Then they would stand trembling as Patrick poured the water over them and placed anointing oil on their foreheads as a symbol of their devotion to God.

Aside from the introduction of Christianity, life in fifth-century Ireland continued much as it had for hundreds of years. Tribes still raided each other for cattle, and occasionally battles were fought, but for the most part the steady rhythm of farm life ruled the land. Outside Ireland the world was more chaotic. By the middle of the fifth century, the Germanic tribes that had entered the Empire were beginning to settle down throughout western Europe. The pagan Franks had moved into the low country of the Rhine delta, while the Visigoths had settled in southwestern Gaul. But in the east, the roving Huns from the steppes of Asia had a new leader, Attila, who ravaged the Balkans and set his sights on the rich lands of Gaul. Only the Roman general Aëtius with his German allies was able to check Attila's advance.

The remnants of the Roman aristocracy in Gaul generally lived in harmony with the assorted Germanic tribes ruling the land. These Germans were no strangers to the Romans. For more than a century they had moved across the Roman borders to serve in the legions, often rising to positions of great power. For a young man growing up in the dark forests of central Germany, service in the Roman army was a common and desirable part of life. The

Roman military provided silver and a chance to see the world — Spain, Africa, even Persia. Many German men spoke Latin well and saw themselves as much a part of the Empire as any Roman senator or nobleman. To the Germans and indeed to many Romans, the period of the Germanic takeover in Gaul was just another phase in Roman history. Instead of taxes to the emperor, a Roman nobleman would pay tribute to a local Gothic or Burgundian lord. Wholesale slaughter was of course bad business for any of the new rulers wishing to benefit from their conquests. An occasional show of force and a small standing army were usually enough to keep life running smoothly.

The Christian Church also continued to grow and prosper. Gaul in fact was an important center of Christian thought and writing during the fifth century. Far from being a land of burned-out villages with barbarians rampaging through the countryside, western Europe after the collapse of the Empire was by and large peaceful and prosperous. City life had declined, to be sure, but that was a process that had started long before Alaric sacked Rome. Even Roman legal traditions were still respected, though with a few colorful additions, such as the Burgundian law that anyone caught stealing a dog had to kiss the hound's rear end in front of the whole village.

In Britain, however, life was growing more difficult. In addition to the ever-threatening Picts and Irish in the north and west, respectively, German warriors less civilized than their cousins in Gaul started to arrive on the eastern coast. Angles, Saxons, Jutes, and Frisians launched almost continuous raids on the island. In the southeast they even began to establish permanent settlements. By the time the last western Roman emperor, Romulus Augustulus, was formally deposed in 476, these tribes had taken over large sections of the country around London and were threatening the rest of Britain. The city councils left over from Roman days were ill-equipped to handle threats on such a grand scale.

In town after town there arose men known as tyrants who gathered together what remained of Roman power and fought to defend the British against external threats. These men resembled the old Celtic chieftains and their bands of violent warriors more than Romans, but they got the job done. If the citizens had to give up a few rights here and there to satisfy the new leaders, it was a small price to pay, so they believed, for security. Many of these tyrants came from the old Romano-British nobility and saw themselves as heroic defenders of civilization against heathen tribes from across the sea. Most of them were Christians as well. The church in Britain, like the rest of society, must have turned a blind eye to any abuses by these tyrants as long as they kept the peace. We know the names of only a few of these rulers, such as Vortigern, Coroticus, and Ambrosius Aurelianus — the last having been a particularly successful general against the Saxons who may have inspired the enduring legend of King Arthur.

To Patrick, these men were only distant names across the Irish Sea. He continued his reports to the church leaders in Britain and received occasional aid and reinforcements from his homeland, but British politics were of little interest to him. British tyrants, after all, were far away and posed no threat to his Irish flock. The shifting powers of Irish kings, by contrast, were keenly important to Patrick as they directly affected his mission.

The raid came in the spring, just as the sea between Britain and Ireland calmed enough to allow easy passage. For decades the Irish had raided across the sea for slaves, forcing the besieged Britons to live in fear. Now the tables would be turned. The aged Patrick had just finished baptizing the latest group of Irish Christians. They were a large clan of several extended families from a tribe on the east coast. The events leading up to Easter — instruction of converts, special religious services, happy celebrations after a long winter — had left him exhausted. He was looking forward to a few days of rest and quiet prayer. The next morning the news came that the newly baptized Christians had been attacked on their way home. Most of the men had been killed. The women and children, some still wearing their baptismal robes and with sweet anointing oil still on their foreheads, had been kidnapped. Apart from a few especially beautiful women, who would be claimed as prizes by Coroticus and his men, they were now on their way to the slave markets of Britain.

We don't know exactly who Coroticus was or where in Britain he ruled. He may be the same man as the prince Ceredig from early Welsh stories, but it is impossible to say for certain. What we do know is that he was a brutal warlord living some-

where on the west coast of Britain.
Coroticus would have been based near the
Irish Sea in order to make such a raid
practicable. He was at least nominally a
Christian, but he and the men gathered
around him made no distinction between
Christian and pagan when it came to slave
raids. The fact that Patrick had just baptized the Irish they attacked meant nothing
to them.

Patrick's letter to Coroticus and his collection of homicidal pirates burns with
such anger and fury that any reader can
tell Patrick could barely control his
seething rage. Murder! The beloved Irish
natives with whom he had worked for so
long, friends he had brought to a faith of
gentleness and kindness, had been brutally
slaughtered or stolen away by his own
countrymen, Romans who professed to be
Christians themselves! The irony was not
lost on Patrick. As a young man from a
Christian family, he had been kidnapped
by pagan Irish raiders and sold into slavery
in a foreign land. He had afterward given
up everything to return to Ireland and lead
his former captors to a new life. Now,
these beloved Irish, made Christians by his
diligent labor, had been killed or stolen

away to the land of his birth.

The remarkable *Letter to the Soldiers of Coroticus* is at the same time a decree of excommunication, a heartfelt plea, a carefully argued sermon, a word of comfort to his Irish followers, and a powerful prayer to God for divine justice. Copies were sent not just to Coroticus but to church leaders in Britain and fellow Christians in Ireland. Patrick begins with a declaration of both his humility and his authority:

> I am Patrick the ignorant sinner and, I declare, a bishop in Ireland — a position I believe I was appointed to by God himself. I am a stranger and an exile living among barbarians and pagans, because God cares for them.

The statement that God cared for the Irish was a crucial assertion. Most Britons were quite prepared to see the Irish as subhuman, fit only for slavery. Countless British men and women had seen their children or friends carried away and their lives shattered by Irish raiders who looked and sounded to them like uncivilized beasts rising from some barbarian Hades. For years Patrick had faced British opposition to his ministry on the simple ground that the Irish were animals not deserving to hear the gospel of Christ. He had to make it clear from the start of the letter that the Irish were every bit as beloved by God as any Briton. In fact, Patrick saw his Irish converts as more civilized than Coroticus and his men. He deliberately refused to grant the British leader and his men the title they so valued: "Notice I don't call you my fellow Romans — no, your crimes have made you citizens of Hell!" Nothing could have stung Coroticus more, which was exactly Patrick's intent. The tyrant saw himself as a preserver of Roman civilization in Britain, a true Roman leader saving his subjects from the barbarian storm raging around the island. Patrick claims just the opposite, classing Coroticus and his men, not the Irish, as subhuman demons.

Patrick had tried reasoning with Coroticus at first:

> The very next day I sent a message to you with a priest I had taught from childhood and some other clergy asking that you return the surviving captives with at least some of their goods — but you only laughed.

The diplomatic approach had failed, so he turned to the one weapon he possessed that might have some effect on Coroticus — his power as a Christian bishop. Coroticus might laugh at Patrick's envoys, but a formal letter from an ordained leader of the church admonishing the British ruler and those around him might shame the tyrant into releasing his captives. Patrick may have learned a thing or two about the power of satire from the Irish bards. In cases when force was not effective, the sting of scorn and condemnation might move even the most hardened heart.

Patrick directs the letter not just at Coroticus and his men but at anyone living under the tyrant's rule. He appeals to the humanity of his fellow Britons and exhorts them to shun those who attacked his Irish flock:

> I most sincerely ask you, my fellow Christians, not to have anything to do with these men — don't eat and drink with them, don't even accept charity from them — until they beg and cry to God to forgive them. They must also free their Christian women and captives.

Like a good Roman lawyer, he then cites numerous precedents for his condemnation.

He assaults the tyrant and his men with a barrage of Scripture, quoting verses condemning murder, theft, greed, covetousness, and hatred. For someone with only a basic education, Patrick knew the Bible very well. Throughout both letters he easily and almost unconsciously weaves passages from the Old and New Testaments into his writing. Often he paraphrases a passage rather than quoting it directly, but sometimes his biblical verses are strange to modern readers because of the text he used. The Vulgate or common Latin Bible of Jerome, which was to dominate the Western Church for many centuries, was just becoming widespread during Patrick's lifetime. He instead often used a simpler and sometimes less accurate text known as the Old Latin Bible. But whatever version Patrick used, he assailed Coroticus with Scripture mercilessly.

Patrick's letter had multiple audiences, not the least of which was God. Of course, Patrick knew Coroticus and his companions were also listening: "God, I know these horrible actions break your heart — even those dwelling in Hell would blush in shame." The tyrant must have squirmed on his throne to hear such prayers. His men, although loyal to their chief, must have begun to question whether this raid had really been such a good idea. It was one thing to anger a few Irishmen or even a distant bishop, but who could hide from the wrath of God?

Patrick takes a final stab at the supposed civilized rule of Coroticus by comparing him unfavorably with the Germans on the continent:

> Do you know what the Roman Christians of Gaul do? They send holy, experienced men to the pagan Franks and other barbarian tribes with great bags of money to ransom Christians who have been captured. But you — you kill them or sell them as slaves to a people who don't even know God. It's as if you sold your fellow Christians to a brothel!

Slave raiding was not restricted to the British Isles. The Germanic tribes across the Rhine had been carrying Gaulish Christians into slavery for years — but they, at least, were open to negotiation. A reasonable deal worked out by shrewd priests would often result in return of the captured men and women. By contrast, Coroticus, in Patrick's eyes, was worse than the barbarians who had brought down the Roman Empire.

Before ending his letter, Patrick writes a stirring lament for the Irish captured and killed during the Easter raid. For those who are still alive but who he fears he will never see again, he cries from the heart:

> With tears and sorrow I will mourn for you, my beautiful, beloved family and children — from the countless number born into Christ through me. What more can I do? How can I help God or my fellow human beings? The wicked with their evil deeds have won. We have been torn apart and separated.

For those killed by Coroticus and his men, he at least knows that their suffering is over:

> Those of my children who were murdered — I weep for you, I weep for you. But I also rejoice in my spirit because my work in Ireland among you was not in vain. Since this hideous, unspeakable crime did happen, I at least thank God that you as baptized Christians have gone to Heaven. I can see you now starting your journey to that place

where there is no more sorrow or death. There you will rejoice and jump for joy just like calves released from their ropes.

For the benefit of Coroticus and his henchmen, Patrick pointedly adds this to the eulogy: "And you will trample down the wicked, for they will be ashes under your feet."

Even though Patrick was seething with righteous anger, he found room in his heart at the letter's conclusion for the possibility of redemption. Once his message had been delivered to the court of Coroticus,

perhaps then, even though late, they will repent of all the evil they have done — these murderers of God's family — and free the Christians they have enslaved. Perhaps then they will deserve to be redeemed and live with God now and forever.

Patrick knew firsthand both the destructive force of sin and the miraculous power of forgiveness. He had long ago abandoned his anger against the Irish who kidnapped him and sold him into slavery. If Patrick had been a different man, if he had not experienced what he believed was the overpowering grace of God, he himself might have been like Coroticus. He had the noble blood, the courage, the determination to have been a formidable tyrant in his native Britain. Patrick could have led devastating raids of revenge and profit against the Irish. He instead returned to the land of his enslavement with the power of faith.

Twelve

Confession

I declare in truth and with joy in my heart — before God and his holy angels — that I have never had any motive in my work except preaching the good news and its promises. That is the only reason I returned here to Ireland — a place I barely escaped alive.

We will never know if Patrick's letter to Coroticus and his soldiers succeeded in restoring the captive Irish Christians to their native land. What we can be reasonably sure of is that the letter infuriated the leaders of the British church. Early church documents state repeatedly that priests and bishops should not interfere with the congregations of other bishops. Church tradition demanded that Patrick contact the bishop of the British town where Coroticus lived and ask him to discipline the wayward tyrant himself.

But there are two reasons this course of

action would not have worked. First, the British bishop who had jurisdiction over Coroticus was not about to chastise such a ruler over a matter not involving British Christians. The church needed Coroticus and his protection as much as did anyone else in Britain. The bishop probably shook his head when he heard of the raid and was genuinely distressed to hear of Christians, even Irish ones, being killed or sold into slavery, but for him to have acted on his misgivings would have caused great difficulties for the local church and its work. The second reason Patrick didn't go through the British church was time. If he had waited while the matter went before a bishop or church council, the captives would have been sold and irretrievably scattered throughout Britain and perhaps beyond. Patrick could not wait for his petition to languish in a committee — he had to directly address Coroticus.

Patrick comments several times in his letters that the bishops of Britain had been a source of trouble for his mission for many years. They had barely allowed him to work in Ireland as a bishop in the first place. Many of them honestly did not think that the Irish were worth saving and couldn't understand why anyone would want to work among them. Once in place Patrick faced continual harassment from British churchmen, especially as his successes grew. Opponents grumbled that he was creating his own fiefdom and that he must be raking in piles of Irish gold as church offerings. And since the beginning many of them had resented the fact that a man with so little education could rise to a position of such power in the church. Back when Ireland was just an undesirable and dangerous backwater, Patrick might have been fit to go there. Hope you keep your head on your shoulders, they must have laughed. But as the church in Ireland grew, many of the British church leaders believed such a successful and potentially lucrative ministry should be handed over to a person of higher standing. Patrick might have done the grunt work, but they wanted to reap the rewards of his labor.

When the letter to Coroticus and his soldiers was read in the churches of Britain, it was more than the bishops could stand. Bad enough that Patrick was holding sway in Ireland, but now he was trying to exercise his authority on subjects of the British church. Never mind that Coroticus and his men were guilty of a horrible crime — it was a matter of principle and fraternal harmony that a bishop should not and could not interfere in church matters outside his jurisdiction. When the bishops read the letter, cringing at its schoolboy Latin, they must have decided it was time for Patrick to go.

By reading the *Confession* closely, we can see what happened next. Patrick was summoned back to Britain to face review. But he knew that if he returned to his homeland, even for a short time, he would never be allowed to continue his work in Ireland. He would be roundly condemned on dubious charges and forced to retire while another man took his place. In Patrick's mind this outcome simply was not acceptable. His many years of labor had built a church that was growing but still fragile. Would a new bishop understand the intricacies of Irish tribal politics? Would he be able to deal with the Druids? Would he support the native Irish priests Patrick had ordained, or would they be pushed aside to make room for the bishop's own men? Would a new church leader understand how precarious the situation was for the women of Ireland, especially the slaves? So much of Patrick's work depended on his personal touch and his extensive contacts built up through decades of careful work.

With a new bishop, the whole church in Ireland might collapse like a house of cards. But in Patrick's letter we also see pride — a justified and understandable pride, but pride nonetheless — as a motivation. He wanted to finish the work he had begun. He had given up everything to come to Ireland. He wanted to labor among his beloved Irish until he drew his last breath. He had nothing to go home to — everything that mattered to him was in Ireland.

Patrick's second letter is traditionally called the *Confession*, but the original document had no title. The name comes from the final line, in which he states that the letter is his *confessio* before death. The Latin word can have the modern meaning of an admission of guilt, but Patrick's letter is actually a defense against charges of corruption brought against him by the British church. It is also a selective story of Patrick's life as well as a testimony to the Irish themselves of his work among them. We may grow frustrated that Patrick doesn't fill in more details of what he was doing before and during his Irish mission, but we must remember that everything he writes of is designed to show that he was chosen by the grace of God to serve selflessly among the Irish. Boyhood, slavery, escape, dreams, threats, temptations — all are included to convince his readers that he, like the apostle Paul, was selected by God and guided by him in his work. We would love to know where Patrick spent his missing years or what he thought of the Irish Druids, but for Patrick, such details are simply not important. Instead of criticizing the *Confession* as a failed autobiography, we have to appreciate the letter for the compelling work that it is.

Patrick's *Confession* is like no other document from ancient times. The Roman orator Cicero wrote dozens of letters to friends and family, but they don't reveal the true person behind the pen. Likewise, St. Augustine's *Confessions* is a carefully constructed spiritual biography that still leaves a reader wondering just what kind of man the author was beneath the ornate and exquisitely organized prose. But in Patrick's *Confession*, unlike in any other contemporary letter, we have a window into the soul of a person.

"I am Patrick — a sinner — the most unsophisticated and unworthy among all the faithful of God. Indeed to many I am the most despised." The opening of the letter immediately engages the reader with its brutal honesty. Patrick writes without pretense or even forethought, from the perspective of his old age, from the great pain he has experienced, and from his heart. He never hesitates to tell his readers his many faults and shortcomings, but he is forthright without being self-pitying. Patrick wants his readers, especially the British bishops, to know that he has nothing to hide. He describes himself as a man who has been through the most degrading of circumstances and seen the worst the human heart can produce, yet he has such faith and hope in the future that readers can't help but be drawn to him.

If organization in the *Confession* seems lacking at times, if Patrick seems to jump from past to present or repeat himself on occasion, we have to remember that he is writing in an informal, conversational style. It's as if we are listening to him as he struggles to work out in his own mind what he wants to say to his critics and friends. Patrick is painfully aware of his lack of literary skill:

I am very ashamed and afraid to show just how awkward my writing is. I am not able to explain things in just a few words like those who can write briefly. My mind and my spirit can't even work together so that my words say what I really feel inside.

But the shortcomings that embarrassed Patrick and annoyed his fellow bishops make him appealing to modern readers. Instead of listening to a Roman lawyer or politician giving an empty speech full of pretense and polished rhetoric, we hear Patrick telling his story in his own simple words.

Even though Patrick is ashamed of his unsophisticated writing, he never hesitates to meet his critics head-on. For years he had faced threats and violence. He had been beaten, enslaved, and continually harassed by Irish warriors and kings, who made the bishops of Britain look like choirboys. Patrick was not about to become a wilting flower when he faced losing his life's work:

Listen to me well, all of you, great and small, everyone who has any fear of God — especially you wealthy land-owners so proud of your education — listen and consider this carefully: God chose foolish little me from among all of you who seem so wise and so expert in the law and so powerful in your eloquence. He picked ignorant Patrick ahead of all of you — even though I am not worthy — he picked me to go forth with fear and reverence — and without any of you complaining at the time — to serve the Irish faithfully.

The leading British churchmen would have been from noble families with extensive estates, but Patrick was not impressed by them. He states clearly at the beginning of the *Confession* that he too was of noble birth and from a landowning family. His father was both a Roman decurion and a Christian deacon, the son of a priest and owner of a prosperous villa. Patricius, son of Calpornius, son of Potitus, was every bit a Roman of the highest class. If he lacked the trappings of nobility, it was because he had freely given up his wealth and status for the benefit of the Irish.

As proof that God chose him and continued to support him in his Irish work, Patrick offers the visions God had granted him over the years. He describes seven revelations and declares that there were many others as well. All came to him in dreams, beginning with the first two when he was still a slave, telling him he would soon be free. Other dreams came at home in Britain and later during his ministry in Ireland, including one the very night he heard of the charges brought against him. But the visions from God that served Patrick in the most practical way were those which he claims to have received regarding upcoming danger during his work among the Irish — a kind of early warning system that would tell him of trouble lying in his path: "God knows everything before it happens, so — with him as my witness — I can tell you he used to warn me frequently of trouble in advance." Patrick knew such claims would not go over well among the sophisticated and skeptical British bishops:

Laugh and make fun of me if you want to — I will not keep quiet, nor will I hide the signs and wonderful things that God has revealed to me many years before they actually happened. For God knew everything that would occur even before the beginning of time.

The churchmen might grant that God had spoken to the prophets and apostles, and perhaps to an occasional saint of exceptional holiness, but they were not about to believe that this troublesome bishop had a direct line to Heaven.

The formal accusations against Patrick began with the unknown sin he had committed as a teenager. Whatever this transgression was, it was enough for the bishops to charge him with long after the fact. The same old friend who had stood up for Patrick when the church leaders were debating whether to appoint him bishop to Ireland betrayed him to the council now. This friend had been with Patrick from his early days in the church and had heard the confession of his boyhood sin before Patrick was even a deacon. What prompted an old comrade to reveal a private matter in public is hard to say — perhaps pressure from the bishops or even jealousy at Patrick's success. Whatever the reason, Patrick never held this breach of trust against his friend.

He realized, however, that this early sin was just a pretense for the more serious accusations to follow — greed, corruption, and getting rich from his Irish converts. He boldly and vigorously refutes these charges:

Among the pagans of Ireland I have lived and will continue to live in honesty and truth. God knows I have cheated none of them — nor would I ever think of doing so.

But he does explain why the peculiar circumstances of Irish culture demanded that he conduct his financial affairs in a way that might anger a council of bishops in faraway Britain. The first problem was the gifts he received from the women of Ireland:

Some of them have been known to offer me small gifts and to place their jewelry on the altar as an offering, but I always returned it to them. They were shocked that I wouldn't accept these gifts.

The bishops were shocked as well, because they saw these donations as legitimate offerings to the church to fund its expenses, in both Ireland and Britain. In their minds Patrick should have taken the gifts, made a careful accounting of them, and sent a portion on to Britain. This was not simple avarice by the bishops but the reality that the Christian Church was an organization like any other, with financial obligations and needs. If Patrick didn't accept these valuable gifts, the work of the church in Ireland and abroad would surely suffer. But he had different ideas:

> I have to take the long-term view on this. I have to be very careful in these matters or some non-Christian might see it as an opportunity to criticize me and my ministry here. I cannot afford to give anyone even the smallest excuse to accuse me or defame my work.

Patrick was aware that he was being closely watched by the pagan political and religious leaders of Ireland. Some were eagerly waiting for a chance to prove the whole Christian movement was just a money-making sham that should be driven from the island. Patrick could not afford even the appearance of corruption and greed if he wanted his mission to proceed with integrity. But the bishops suspected him of taking these gifts and keeping them for himself. How could anyone, to their minds, turn down such offerings? But Patrick answers emphatically that he never accepted the gifts offered to him by the women of Ireland. He also never took a single coin or even, as he says, a pair of shoes from his baptized converts.

Patrick boldly states to the bishops and his own Irish followers that he used church funds to bribe the Irish kings to receive him and paid their sons so that he could travel between tribes:

> You all know very well how I paid out this money to those in power in those regions I have visited frequently. I've probably paid out enough to buy fifteen slaves. . . . I'm not sorry that I paid out bribes — in fact, I'm not finished yet. I spend money now and will spend even more.

The price of fifteen slaves was more than the honor price of an Irish king, a huge outlay for a struggling church. Even spread out over a number of years, it's easy to see why the British bishops objected to such an unconventional use of money. Paying taxes and tithes they understood, but giving church money to savages merely to roam the Irish countryside freely was beyond them. If Patrick wasn't pocketing the money supposedly spent on these kings, he was at least wasting the church resources in an outrageous manner. In their minds, the leadership of the church in Ireland and the financial potential of the growing Irish Christian community simply had to be brought under the control of the British church.

And so, to answer his critics, to comfort his Irish followers, and to make his final testimony to God, Patrick composed his *Confession*. We can imagine him, when he finished the letter, sitting at his small wooden desk surrounded by a few of his faithful priests. If any of his assistants were from Britain or Gaul, as later stories relate, perhaps one with education and scribal training humbly offered to review the letter and shape it into a more polished ecclesiastical document, such as the bishops were accustomed to. No, Patrick would have said, it is the declaration of my life. It must be in my words, however crude they may sound to the bishops. Let God judge if I am worthy to remain here among you.

We don't know for certain the outcome of the charges against Patrick. We have no record that he was removed from office, and it seems unlikely that he left voluntarily. His fondest wish and his final plea to the British bishops was that he be allowed to remain in Ireland:

If I have ever done anything worthwhile for the God I love, I ask that I might be allowed to die here for his name with these converts and slaves — even if it means that I won't have a marked grave or that my body is torn apart piece by piece by dogs or wild animals or that I serve as a meal for the birds of the air.

The *Confession* ends with the heartfelt appeal of an old man that he be allowed to finish his task and live out what remains of his life among his beloved Irish.

Thirteen

Ireland After Patrick

I must choose to proclaim the gift of
God and his everlasting help confidently and without fear, to make known
his name everywhere, so that even after
I die it might be a kind of spiritual
legacy left behind for my brothers and
sons, so many thousands I baptized for
God.

Patrick's wish for an unmarked grave was
prophetic. In an age obsessed with saints,
relics, and pilgrimage sites, no one knew for
certain where Patrick died and was buried.
Indeed, for over a century after his death,
few people remembered that he had been
alive. While other saints were venerated soon
after their deaths and attracted large follow-
ings, Patrick slipped into obscurity. We don't
even know the year of his death. Irish annals
written long after the fact place his death in
the 460s or 490s, but all the dates are later
calculations of little independent value.

We know so little about the details of Patrick's life that it seems fitting his death should be a mystery as well. He probably would have wanted it that way — his letters tell of a humble man who deflected any glory away from himself. When the popularity of Patrick grew in later centuries, enterprising churchmen invented a final resting place for him at Downpatrick, south of Belfast, but this location is no more certain than any other. Even the traditional date of his death, March 17, St. Patrick's Day, is little more than a guess.

No one knows whether Patrick returned to Britain after writing the *Confession* or whether his wish to visit the Christians of Gaul ever came true. No one knows if Patrick's final years were calm or troubled. Perhaps he did meet his end as he prophesied — murdered by greedy warriors or a hotheaded king during his journeys around the Irish countryside. Perhaps he passed away peacefully in bed surrounded by the grandchildren of his first converts. In either case, Patrick would have accepted it as the will of God. What mattered to him was only that he be allowed to die in Ireland.

Christianity in Ireland did not perish along with Patrick, but we have so few details of this early period of Irish history that it is extraordinarily difficult to say what happened to the church he founded. We do know that later stories of Patrick converting every soul in Ireland are plainly false. Druids, Celtic gods, and traditional religion lasted for at least another two centuries, perhaps longer. Nor did peace reign over Ireland with the coming of Christianity. Kings and armies still fought with all the bloody vigor of their pagan ancestors.

The information we do have about Irish Christianity in the years after Patrick comes from a few ancient poems, fragmentary church documents, and partly fictional lives of saints. These sources give us an often distorted and incomplete picture, but at least they provide the earliest Irish views on the life and work of Patrick himself. They are poor evidence for the Patrick of history, but they are important testimony to the Patrick of myth.

One hymn in Latin praising Patrick was attributed to Secundinus, supposedly a companion who worked with Patrick on his missionary efforts. The poem has twenty-three stanzas, each starting with a new letter of the Latin alphabet in order. It begins with *Audite* (Listen):

Listen everyone, all you who love God,
   to the holy qualities
of that blessed man of Christ, Patrick
   the bishop.
He is like the holy angels in his wonderful
   ways
and equal to the apostles because of his
   perfect life.

The Latin is old, but the hymn is so full of overflowing adoration that it's hard to believe the self-effacing Patrick of the letters would have approved of such a work. Secundinus's hymn in fact probably dates to the century after Patrick and shows that Patrick had a small following after his death. But even at this early date the man we see proclaimed as God's glorious messenger to the heathen has little to do with the Patrick of the *Confession*. What we discover in this hymn is the beginning of a cult being built around the memory of Patrick. Later stories say that the hymn could be used as a prayer of protection against evil and that anyone who sang it on the day of his or her death would be saved by the intercession of Patrick himself.

Another important source on Christianity in early Ireland is a document known as the *First Synod of St. Patrick*. It claims to be a set of rules for Christian living endorsed by Patrick himself. Some scholars have accepted it as genuine, but it more likely dates from the seventh rather than the fifth century. Even so, in its thirty-five rules we can see the concerns of Irish church leaders of this period. Ironically, the document frequently condemns priests and bishops who interfere in matters outside their appointed areas — exactly as Patrick did with Coroticus and his men. The penalty for such acts was excommunication. The synod also warns against priests and proclaimed virgins of Christ who stray from the path of sexual purity. For example, priests and nuns, to avoid temptation, were never to stay in the same inn or even ride in a chariot together. But some of the most interesting and revealing passages deal with relations between Christians and non-Christians — a clear indication that many pagans still existed. Priests were to be held to a high standard of behavior in their dealings with non-Christians:

Let no member of the clergy guarantee the pledge of a pagan in any amount. If this happens and the pagan defaults on the agreement through trickery, as is often the case, the priest shall pay the penalty out of his own pocket. If the priest fights a duel with the pagan who tricked him, he shall be excommunicated.

In addition, no Christians were to have dealings with Druids or to appeal to secular authorities over the Church.

As Ireland was a totally rural island, the normal church organization found in Britain and continental Europe could not be applied. In areas under Roman rule, a bishop was headquartered in a city or town and from there had jurisdiction over the surrounding countryside. In the absence of urban centers, the monasteries that grew up in Ireland in the sixth and seventh centuries became the centers of Christian life and church government. One of these was founded in Kildare, west of Dublin, by a remarkable woman. Brigid of Kildare was born sometime in the late fifth century and perhaps knew Patrick as a child. We know very little of the historical Brigid and so are forced to look to the later stories of her life to glean bits and pieces of her true story amid the standard miracles attributed to Christian saints and the influences of Celtic mythology.

Some stories say Brigid was born of Christian parents, but others relate that her mother was a Christian slave and her father a pagan. Either could be the case, but the latter fits nicely with Patrick's reports of numerous Christian slave women in fifth-century Ireland. As with all good Christian saints of her sex in such stories, Brigid longed to be a virgin of God and chose the path of chastity early in her youth. She desired to establish a church and monastery at Kildare, but knowing she could not accomplish this alone as a woman, she persuaded a hermit priest to rule with her as a bishop. The *Life of Brigid*, written by the priest Cogitosus in the early seventh century, claims that Kildare excelled all the other monasteries in Ireland and ruled over most of them as well. This was a deliberate challenge to Armagh in the north, which claimed exactly the same thing.

Brigid's reported miracles often involve her power over animals, cattle, pigs, and even foxes. It's likely that these stories incorporate elements of tales drawn from earlier Irish goddesses, as do the miracles claiming control over rivers and streams.

The wonderful tale of Brigid hanging her wet cloak on a sunbeam to dry is another clear borrowing from myth. But such stories shouldn't be dismissed simply as baseless folktales or cynical efforts of the Church to replace paganism with a barely distinguishable Christian alternative. These tales instead show the Irish actively participating in the transition from a non-Christian to a Christian worldview by preserving their native heritage as part of the new religion. They would have been deeply offended by any suggestion that elements drawn from Celtic myth made Brigid or any other saint less Christian. It was simply a Christianity embraced on their own terms.

Early Irish Christians were deeply impressed both by the stories of faithful martyrs perishing under Roman cruelty and by the lives of holy hermits in the deserts of Egypt and Syria. Having neither Romans nor deserts, those Irish who wished to imitate the sacrifice and solitude of the Christian past often chose the rocky islets off the western coast for their own form of living martyrdom. On these almost inaccessible points of land, the monks would build simple stone huts and endure deprivations in this life as a preparation for the next. Some Irish ascetics traveled far indeed. Reliable stories say that when the Vikings arrived in Iceland they found Irish monks.

The most famous story of an Irish monk sailing to the west in search of enlightenment is the *Voyage of St. Brendan*. Like Brigid, the historic Brendan is poorly known but was probably born in the late fifth century, just as Patrick's life was coming to an end. He founded several monasteries in southwest Ireland and was revered as a wise abbot. The story of his travels to the west is fiction drawing on similar tales in Celtic myth, but his voyage does give us a marvelous feel for the relationships between members of a religious order in early Ireland. The Brendan of our tale is an unquestioned leader who provides a kind word of guidance or a spiritual kick in the pants to his followers as needed. Many have tried to tie locations mentioned in the *Voyage* to real places, even North America, but success in this effort is no more likely than discovering the cave of Homer's one-eyed Cyclops. The islands Brendan and his companions visit are significant only as metaphorical places. Whether they are landing on the back of a giant fish or visiting the Promised Land of the Saints during their seven-year trip, these monks are always on a pilgrimage of spiritual growth.

One of the best episodes in the *Voyage of Brendan* begins when the travelers spy in the distance what seems to be a figure sitting on a small, storm-battered rock. This wretched man turns out to be none other than Judas Iscariot, who betrayed Jesus. In Brendan's tale, Judas is actually on a brief vacation from Hell, granted by the mercy of Christ. He begs Brendan to beseech God on his behalf so that he might be allowed to remain on his tiny rock a few more hours. Though fierce demons threaten Brendan and his men, the abbot intercedes for Judas, and his wish is granted. By contrast, in Dante's *Inferno*, Judas is the worst of all sinners, gnawed on headfirst by Satan himself in never-ending torture. Brendan's attitude toward Judas reflects a remarkable mercy seen in the early Irish Church, which held that every sin could be forgiven, though the price might be heavy. The Irish were well known for their contributions to the idea of penance in Christian theology, which carefully explained how sins might be atoned for with sincere actions of repentance — the greater the sin, the harder the atonement.

It's no coincidence that such a system developed in a land in which there was a stipulated honor price for every person and a prescribed method of payment for any crime against one's neighbor or king. To the Irish churchmen, God was the greatest king of all, and his honor price demanded a steep but limited payment for sin — not in cattle or gold, though this was sometimes the case, but through fasting, prayer, and other means of atonement.

In the late sixth century, only a hundred years after Patrick's death, Christianity was well enough established in Ireland that many clergy felt the need to spread the gospel to even more distant areas. Others wanted to carry Irish forms of monastic life nearer the center of the Christian world. These pilgrims for Christ saw their voluntary exile from the shores of Ireland as a living martyrdom just as did those monks who perched themselves on wave-pounded islets in the vast Atlantic. To leave Ireland was to leave the only home they had ever known, just as Patrick had left his home in Britain willingly to serve in Ireland. These monks took with them the traditions and learning they had received in their Irish monasteries. Some went to the pagan Picts and Saxons, others to long-Christianized areas of the old Roman Empire. Those who went to Gaul and Italy did not return bearing the forgotten fruits of classical learning. The Irish did not save civilization — it had never been lost. The vibrant monasteries and learned nobility of western Europe, not to mention the entire eastern Roman Empire, would have laughed at the notion that the Irish were rescuing them from barbarism. They respected the learning of the Irish as they would the scholarship of any worthy visitors, but the Gauls and Italians had only to pull Virgil or Cicero from their shelves if they wanted to drink from the fountain of classical wisdom. What the Irish who settled in Europe were known and admired for was their careful scholarship and fierce dedication to the rigors of monastic life.

One of the first to leave Ireland was Colum Cille, better known by his Latin name, Columba. Like Patrick he left behind his noble status to travel to a remote land, the island of Iona in the Scottish Hebrides. Though not so far in miles from his home, it was a world away from the thriving Christian life of Ireland. In 563 Columba founded on Iona a monastery that became a powerful force in the conversion of the Picts in Scotland and ultimately in the introduction of Christianity to the pagan Saxons of northern Britain. Columba's life story, composed by his relative Adomnán, contains many of the familiar miracles and wonder tales attributed to Christian saints, but it also has a valuable core of historic facts. Adomnán himself is worthy of note as a churchman of high principle who in the late seventh century enacted a document known as the Law of Innocents, protecting women and children from the ravages of Irish wars.

In the early seventh century, St. Fursa traveled from eastern Ireland to northern Gaul to establish monasteries. But Columbanus is perhaps the best known of the early Irish pilgrims to the continent because of his surviving letters. Columbanus traveled first to Gaul and established several monasteries under a strict rule, eventually ending his life at the monastery of Bobbio in northern Italy. His teachings helped establish clear and firm rules of monastic order in Europe for generations. Columbanus also corresponded with leading figures of his day, such as Pope Boniface IV. In 613 he sent a letter boldly urging the Pope to maintain orthodox teachings, as had the Irish:

We Irish who live at the ends of the earth are followers of Saints Peter and Paul and all those who wrote the Scriptures under the direction of the Holy Spirit. We teach nothing beyond the truth revealed in the Gospels and by the Apostles. There are no heretics living on our island, no Jews, no one straying from the true faith — our adherence to the universal faith is firm. We teach it exactly as it came first from the bishops of Rome, the successors of the Apostles.

Columbanus may be referring to the mission of Palladius, sent to Ireland by Pope Celestine. In any case, though Columbanus never mentions Patrick, he is proud of the orthodoxy of Irish Christianity maintained from the earliest days.

In the travels of Columba, Fursa, Columbanus, and many others, the work of Patrick came full circle. Two centuries earlier a young Roman nobleman had been kidnapped by Irish slave traders and carried off to an island that barely knew the teachings of Christianity. With the pilgrimages of the Irish saints to Britain and the continent, Patrick's mission was completed as the descendants of his Irish converts themselves carried Christianity to known and unknown lands.

One final piece of writing from early Ireland must be mentioned. It is a prayer not in Latin but in Old Irish that shows how the new religion had bridged not only the culture but also the language of early Ireland. Irish poetry and prose was among the first non-Latin literature to be recorded in western Europe. Long before the English of *Beowulf* or the Norse of the Icelandic sagas, the Irish monks were preserving ancient Celtic stories and recording Christian teachings in their native tongue.

The *Breastplate* of Patrick — *Lorica* in Latin, in Irish the *Fáeth Fiada* — is a morning song of praise and invocation. From the earliest times it has been attributed to Patrick, but it was probably composed at least a century after his death. Even so, it is a stirring prayer full of nature imagery, calling on the Trinity for guidance and protection against all manner of evils — including the spells of women (probably witches), blacksmiths (who in Celtic society were thought to have supernatural powers), and Druids. I have translated the prayer very literally, preserving as closely as possible its original structure and tremendous power. Though it was probably not written by Patrick, it certainly captures the spirit of the man we see in his letters:

I rise today
with a mighty power, calling on the Trinity,
with a belief in the threeness,
with a faith in the oneness
of the creator of creation.

I rise today
with the power of Christ's birth and
baptism,
with the power of his crucifixion and
burial,
with the power of his resurrection and
ascension,
with the power of his return for the
final judgment.

I rise today
with the power of the love of the
cherubim,
in obedience of angels,
in service of archangels,
in hope of the resurrection and reward,
in the prayers of the patriarchs,
in the foretelling of the prophets,
in the preaching of the apostles,

in the faith of the confessors,
in the innocence of the holy virgins,
in the deeds of righteous men.

I rise today
 with the strength of the sky,
 with the light of the sun,
 with the splendor of the moon,
 with the brilliance of fire,
 with the blaze of lightning,
 with the swiftness of wind,
 with the depth of the ocean,
 with the firmness of earth,
 with the strength of rock.

I rise today
 with the power of God to guide me,
 with the strength of God to raise me,
 with the wisdom of God to lead me,
 with the vision of God to see for me,
 with the ears of God to hear for me,
 with the words of God to speak for me,
 with the hand of God to protect me,
 with the path of God before me,
 with the shield of God to guard me,
 with the friendship of God to keep me
   safe from
  the contriving of demons,
  the temptations of sin,
  the inclinations of my nature,

and everyone who wishes me harm,
   far and near,
   alone and in the crowd.

I summon today all those powers to
      protect me
   against every cruel force which may
         attack my body and soul,
   against the incantations of false prophets,
   against the evil laws of unbelievers,
   against the false laws of the heretics,
   against the subtle temptations of idolatry,
   against the magic of women, blacksmiths,
      and Druids,
   against every knowledge which corrupts
      body and soul.

Christ protect me today
   from poison and burning,
   from drowning and wounding,
   so that I might gain an abundant reward.
      Christ with me, Christ before me,
         Christ behind me,
      Christ in me, Christ below me,
         Christ above me,
      Christ to the right of me, Christ to the
         left of me,
      Christ where I lie, Christ where I sit,
         Christ where I stand,
      Christ in the heart of everyone who
         thinks of me,

246

Christ in the mouth of everyone who
speaks of me,
Christ in every eye which sees me,
Christ in every ear which hears me.

I rise today
with a mighty power, calling on the Trinity,
with a belief in the threeness,
with a faith in the oneness
of the creator of creation.

Epilogue

Patrick's Letters

Stroll down Grafton Street in Dublin past the busy shops and hordes of tourists and you will soon come to the gates of Trinity College. Enter the peaceful grounds of this oldest of Irish universities and you will see the Old Library with its magnificent Long Room full of books from floor to ceiling. In the lower exhibition area lies the justly famous *Book of Kells* with its profusely decorated gospel pages, considered by many to be the most beautifully illuminated manuscript in the world. In a dark corner of the same room, often overlooked by visitors, is a small and comparatively dull-looking manuscript known as the *Book of Armagh*. Inside the fragile pages of this book is the oldest surviving copy of the *Confession*, written out by the scribe Ferdomnach around the year 807, more than three centuries after the death of Patrick.

We can no longer read the original letters of Patrick. Somehow between Viking raids, gnawing rodents, fires, floods, and general carelessness, the two documents written in Patrick's own hand were lost or destroyed. It's remarkable that the *Confession* and *Letter to the Soldiers of Coroticus* survived at all. The *Book of Armagh* contains one of only seven copies of Patrick's letters that have been preserved to the present day. These precious manuscripts are our only links to the genuine Patrick who lived more than fifteen centuries ago. They are copies of copies of his original two letters reproduced by monastic scribes in medieval Europe. As with any document copied repeatedly, mistakes and omissions crept in, so that the surviving manuscripts of Patrick's letters differ in subtle and not so subtle ways. Aside from the *Book of Armagh* in Dublin, the other six manuscripts are in the National Library in Paris, the municipal libraries of Arras and Rouen in northern France, the British Library in London, and two at Salisbury Cathedral in southern England. Each has its unique and sometimes troubled history.

The *Book of Armagh*, even though it is the oldest manuscript, is not necessarily the best for discovering the original text of Patrick's letters. To begin with, it omits entirely the *Letter to the Soldiers of Coroticus* and leaves out significant portions of the *Confession*. The missing parts of the *Confession* are frequently the sections in which Patrick appears most human and least saintlike — the passages in which he admits his weaknesses and failings. It seems likely that the scribes and authorities at Armagh wanted to present a Patrick who better fit their own model of what a saint should be. Why the letter to Coroticus and his men is omitted is more of a mystery. It doesn't make Patrick look bad at all; rather it shows him at his strongest, fighting evil and exerting his authority — qualities the churchmen of Armagh would have prized. Thus the shorter letter was probably not deliberately left out but rather lost to the scribes at Armagh sometime during the three centuries between Patrick's original composition and the year Ferdomnach made his copy.

The *Book of Armagh* sat quietly on a library shelf until, in the year 937, an Irish king recognized its immense value and ordered it enshrined and placed in a leather case. In 1004 a priest recorded on a blank page of the manuscript that Brian Boru, high king of Ireland, visited Armagh and affirmed the privileges of that church. A century later an Armagh clergyman angry at being replaced briefly ran away with the manuscript in a huff. It was then decided that such an important book needed a special protector, so a man was chosen who became known as the *Maor na Canóine* (Keeper of the Book). The position was hereditary, so his descendants bore the responsibility for guarding the book for centuries thereafter. Anyone today with the name MacMaoir or MacMoyre (son of the Keeper) is a member of this family.

Hard times fell on Ireland with the English incursions of the seventeenth century; in 1680 Florence MacMoyre, last of the hereditary Keepers of the Book, pawned it for five pounds. The book changed hands several times before ending up in the Royal Irish Academy in 1846. Seven years later the archbishop of Armagh purchased the manuscript and presented it to Trinity College, where it remains to this day.

Much less is known about the history of the other six manuscripts of Patrick's letters. The best evidence suggests that all of them derive from a single copy of both letters that arrived on the continent in the early seventh century. The letters were copied and recopied by scribes and deposited in monasteries in northern France. The Paris manuscript, dating to the tenth century, is the earliest complete copy of both letters. This small volume was part of the abbey library at Saint-Corneille in nearby Compiègne until Napoleon's minister of the interior confiscated it in 1802 and sent it to Paris. It has survived the centuries beautifully, unlike the manuscripts from Arras and Rouen. The Arras volume lost parts in the seventeenth century, while the Rouen manuscript is a crumbling fragment preserving only the first pages of the *Confession*. The manuscripts in England, preserving both letters, derive from earlier French copies and date to the eleventh and twelfth centuries.

Though Patrick's letters survived, they were never well known. The Irishman Muirchú, who wrote the first biography of Patrick about 650, had access, if not to copies of Patrick's letters, at least to some source that contained parts of them. In the writing of Muirchú, amid the fanciful miracles of a wonder-working Patrick and the comical transformation of the tyrant Coroticus into a fox as punishment for his evil raid, we see only glimpses of the real Patrick known from his letters.

Bishop Tírechán, who wrote soon after Muirchú, gives an imaginative and elaborate account in which Patrick arrives on the island accompanied by a vast entourage of bishops, priests, deacons, and exorcists. He travels the land founding churches, performing miracles, and ordaining hundreds of bishops, but little of the historical Patrick shines through in Tírechán's story either. Others — Nennius, William of Malmesbury, Jocelin of Furness — wrote of Patrick in the following centuries, but their work is fiction meant to inspire Christians to a heavenly life, not to describe accurately the labors of a fifth-century Roman missionary.

Copies of Patrick's letters did survive, however, and as they spread to France and Britain, they were occasionally read by a curious monk. Patrick was moderately well known throughout the Middle Ages, but only via the fanciful tales of Muirchú and similar stories. Almost no one knew the genuine writings of Patrick himself.

His letters were finally rediscovered in the seventeenth century by churchmen in France and the British Isles. The Irish bishop James Ussher, best known for dating the creation of the world precisely to 4004 B.C., consulted the letters. James Ware, a Protestant minister, produced the first scholarly edition of Patrick's letters in 1656, using the manuscripts from Ireland and England. The French Catholic clergyman Denis discovered the manuscript of Patrick's letters at Arras, and published them in 1668.

Patrick's letters were restricted to those who read Latin until the nineteenth century, when the first English translations appeared. In the last hundred years more than a dozen editions of the letters have been published. In spite of this proliferation, the writings of Patrick are poorly known to this day. Everyone has heard of St. Patrick, of course, but the man most people know is little more than an icon who drove the snakes out of Ireland. This lack of knowledge about the real Patrick is truly regrettable, because he has such an amazing story to tell: a tale of slavery and brutality, pain and self-doubt, sorrow and constant struggle, but ultimately of perseverance, hope, and faith. His letters, in the end, remain as a remarkable gift from an extraordinary man.

I have included a complete translation of Patrick's two letters so that readers can examine these unique documents for themselves. I have tried to be faithful to the original Latin yet convey a sense of the informal but vigorous style in which Patrick writes.

Letter to the Soldiers of Coroticus

I am Patrick the ignorant sinner and, I declare, a bishop in Ireland — a position I believe I was appointed to by God himself. I am a stranger and an exile living among barbarians and pagans, because God cares for them. God is my witness that this is the truth.

I don't like to use forceful words or harsh language, but I will do it because the anger of God and the truth of Christ force me to. I do it for the love of my neighbors here in Ireland and for my spiritual children. I have traded in my homeland, my family, and my very life for them — even if it means my death. If I am worthy, I will devote the rest of my days to teaching the Irish — even if some of you beyond this island despise me.

With my own hands I write this letter — given to my messenger, carried on its way, and handed over to you, the soldiers of Coroticus. Notice I don't call you "my fellow Romans" — no, your crimes have made you citizens of Hell!

You live like the worst barbarians, including your Pictish friends. Blood, blood, blood! Your hands drip with the blood of the innocent Christians you have murdered — the very Christians I nourished and brought to God.

My newly baptized converts, still in their white robes, the sweet smell of the anointing oil still on their foreheads — you murdered them, cut them down with your swords!

The very next day I sent a message to you with a priest I had taught from childhood and some other clergy asking that you return the surviving captives with at least some of their goods — but you only laughed.

I'm not sure who I should pity more — those murdered, the captives you took, or you who have been enslaved by the devil. You will indeed be captives with him forever in Hell, since everyone who enjoys sin is a slave and is called a child of Satan.

Therefore, let everyone who fears God know that these murderers are enemies to me and to Christ my God — the one I serve as an ambassador.

They have killed their own fathers and brothers in Christ! These wolves devour the people of God as if they were eating bread! As the Scripture says: "The wicked have destroyed your law, O Lord." And God in his great kindness had just recently planted this law in Ireland, where it had been growing by his grace.

I am not overstepping my authority. I am one of those God has called and chosen to preach the good news, even in the most difficult of times, to the very ends of the earth. The devil shows his jealousy of our success through the tyrant Coroticus — a man who has no respect for God or his priests. We were selected by God and given a great, divine, and awesome power — to make judgments here on earth that have the authority of God himself.

So I most sincerely ask you, my fellow Christians, not to have anything to do with these men — don't eat and drink with them, don't even accept charity from them — until they beg and cry to God to forgive them. They must also free their Christian women and captives. Remember, Christ died and was crucified for these people.

Listen to Scripture:
- God hates the gifts of evil people. If someone offers a sacrifice stolen

from the poor, it's as if he is sacrificing a son right in front of his father.

- Whoever gains riches unjustly, God vomits him out of his mouth, the angel of death hauls him off, he is tortured by angry dragons, snakes bite him to death, and an ever-burning fire consumes him.
- Woe to those who take what is not theirs.
- How does it help someone if he gains all the riches of the world but loses his own soul?

It would take far too long to list and discuss every instance in Scripture explaining why such horrible actions are wrong, but here are just a few more:

- Greed is a deadly sin.
- Do not desire your neighbor's property.
- Do not murder.
- No murderer can be with Christ.
- Whoever hates his brother is a murderer.
- Whoever does not love his brother remains in spiritual death.

If all this is true, imagine how much

worse it is to bathe in the blood of God's own children — the Irish who only recently have come to know God by my humble effort.

Did I come to Ireland just because I wanted to, without God's direction? Did someone force me to come here? God's spirit ordered me here, far away from my family.

Was it my idea to feel God's love for the Irish and to work for their good? These people once enslaved me and devastated my father's household!

I am of noble birth — the son of a Roman decurion — but I sold my nobility. I'm not ashamed of it and I don't regret it because I did it to help others. Now I am a slave of Christ to a foreign people — but this time for the unspeakable glory of eternal life in Christ Jesus our master.

If my own British countrymen don't respect me, I can only reply that a prophet isn't honored in his own land. Aren't we all part of the same flock? Isn't God the father of us all? Remember that God says: "Whoever isn't with me is against me, and whoever doesn't harvest with me scatters." It isn't right that some people destroy while others build.

I'm not doing all this work for my own satisfaction but for God. He gives me consolation in my heart that I am one of those hunters and fishermen of souls who he says would come in the last days.

God, these soldiers despise me and have ignored my appeals — what can I do? My flock has been torn to pieces and scattered by these wicked men, under the orders of the evil-minded Coroticus.

God, these men who have handed over Christians to their Irish and Pictish allies are far away from you. They have become like hungry wolves who glut themselves on your flock. And your work has been going so well in Ireland — countless sons and daughters of Irish kings are becoming brothers and virgins for Christ.

God, I know these horrible actions break your heart — even those dwelling in Hell would blush in shame.

Christians should be ashamed to enjoy the parties and dinners of these evil men. They live by plunder, filling their houses with loot stolen from dead Christians. These poor fools don't know that the food they serve their friends and their own sons is deadly poison — just as Eve didn't know that she was handing death to her husband, Adam. This is the way it is with all who commit evil acts. They will suffer death as an eternal punishment.

Do you know what the Roman Christians of Gaul do? They send holy, experienced men to the pagan Franks and other barbarian tribes with great bags of money to ransom Christians who have been captured. But you — you kill them or sell them as slaves to people who don't even know God. It's as if you sold your fellow Christians to a brothel!

What hope is there for you or those who flatter you? God will judge you all. As Scripture says: "Not only those who do evil but even those who go along with them will be damned."

I don't know what more I can say about those murdered children of God — those brutally killed by the sword. Scripture says: "Weep with those who weep," and again: "If one of you is crying, let everyone cry."

We as Christians also cry out and weep bitterly for our sons and daughters who were not killed but who were taken and carried off to distant lands. They are in evil places where horrible sins are practiced openly and abundantly. Freeborn people, Christians, sold into slavery! Worst of all, some have been sold to the wicked, godless, abominable Picts!

With tears and sorrow I will mourn for you, my beautiful, beloved family and children — from the countless number born into Christ through me. What more can I do? How can I help God or my fellow human beings? The wicked with their evil deeds have won. We have been torn apart and separated.

Maybe these pirates don't know that we all share the same baptism. Don't they know that the same God is father of us all? No, they hate you — they hate us — because we are Irish. But it is written: "Do you not have one God? Why has each of you turned your back on your neighbor?"

And those of my children who were murdered — I weep for you, I weep for you. But I also rejoice in my spirit because my work in Ireland among you was not in vain. Since this hideous, unspeakable crime did happen, I at least thank God that you as baptized Christians have gone to Heaven. I can see you now starting on your journey to that place where there is no more sorrow or death. There you will rejoice and jump with joy just like calves released from their ropes. And you will trample down the wicked, for they will be ashes under your feet.

You will rule with the apostles, prophets, and martyrs in an eternal kingdom. As Christ himself says: "They will come from the east and west to dine with Abraham, Isaac, and Jacob in the kingdom of heaven. Outside will be dogs, sorcerers, murderers, liars, and those who swear falsely — all these will suffer in a pool of eternal fire." As the apostle says with good reason: "If the righteous are barely safe, where do sinners and those who scornfully break the law think they will end up?"

So, Coroticus, you and your wicked servants, where do you think you will end up? You have treated baptized Christian women like prizes to be handed out, all for the sake of the here and now — this brief, fleeting world. All this will vanish soon, like smoke or clouds — as lying sinners will vanish from the presence of God. The just, however, will happily feast with Christ. They will judge the whole world and forever will rule over wicked kings — Amen.

I declare before God and his angels that

it will be as he has revealed it to me, even though I'm not worthy. This letter, which I have written in Latin, speaks not with my words but with those of God, the apostles, and the prophets — and they do not lie. Whoever believes them will be saved, but whoever ignores them will be condemned. God has spoken.

I implore you, those among you who are servants of God, be courageous and deliver this letter everywhere. Please don't suppress it or conceal it from anyone. Instead, read it to everyone — even to Coroticus himself. Perhaps then God will inspire him so that he and his men will come to their senses and make things right with God. Perhaps then, even though late, they will repent of all the evil they have done — these murderers of God's family — and free the Christians they have enslaved. Perhaps then they will deserve to be redeemed and live with God now and forever.

I hope that you will all find the peace of the Father, Son, and Holy Spirit — Amen.

Confession

I am Patrick — a sinner — the most unsophisticated and unworthy among all the faithful of God. Indeed, to many I am the most despised.

My father was Calpornius, a deacon of the Church, and my grandfather was Potitus, a priest. His home was the village of Bannaventa Berniae, but he also had a country estate nearby. There I was captured when I was just short of my sixteenth birthday, at a time when I had no real knowledge of God. I was led away as a slave to Ireland as were so many thousands of others. We deserved slavery — for we had abandoned God and did not follow his ways. We ignored the warnings of our priests, who pleaded with us again and again to be mindful of our eternal souls. So God poured out his anger on us and scattered us among the hordes of barbarians who live at the edge of the world. And indeed, here today, they can see how unimportant I am.

But it was here in Ireland that God first opened my heart, so that — even though it was a late start — I became aware of my failings and began to turn with my whole heart to the Lord my God. For he looked down on my miserable condition and had compassion for me, young and foolish as I was. He cared for me before I even knew who he was, before I could tell the difference between right and wrong. He protected me and loved me even as a father does his own child.

Because of this I cannot — I will not — be silent. I will tell of the great blessings God has granted to me and the grace he has shown to me in this land of slavery. Because this is the way we should behave toward God — when he has shown us why we were wrong and we have admitted our sins, we should praise him and proclaim his kindness to everyone in the world.

There is no other God — there never was and there never will be. God our father was not born nor did he have any beginning. God himself is the beginning of all things, the very one who holds all things together, as we have been taught.

And we proclaim that Jesus Christ is his son, who has been with God in spirit always, from the beginning of time and before the creation of the world — though in a way we cannot put into words. Through him everything in the universe was created, both what we can see and what is invisible. He was born as a human being and he conquered death, rising into the heavens to be with God. And God gave to him power greater than any creature of the heavens or earth or under the earth, so that someday everyone will declare that Jesus Christ is Lord and God. We believe in him and we wait for him to return very soon. He will be the judge of the living and the dead, rewarding every person according to their actions.

And God has generously poured out on us his Holy Spirit as a gift and a token of immortality. This Spirit makes all faithful believers into children of God and brothers and sisters of Christ.

This we proclaim. We worship one God in three parts, by the sacred name of the Trinity.

God has said through his prophet: "Call on me when you are in trouble and I will rescue you and you will praise me." And again he says: "It is right to declare and make known the deeds of God." So, even though I am far from perfect, I want my brothers and my family to know what kind of person I am — I want them truly to understand the longing of my soul.

I know very well the warning found in the Psalms: "God will destroy those who speak lies." And again in Scripture: "A mouth which lies kills the spirit." God also speaks in the gospel when he says: "On the day of judgment, each person will have to defend every careless word spoken."

Because of this I have been terrified of my judgment on that day when not one of us will be able to hide ourselves away but each of us will have to answer for even the smallest of our sins before the tribunal of the Lord Christ.

I have thought about writing this letter for a long time, but I kept putting it off until now. I have been afraid that people would laugh at the way I write. You see, I don't have much education compared to other people. I was not able to study both literature and theology year after year as they did. They never had to learn to speak any new language but could steadily improve their own Latin until it was practically perfect. But I write Latin as if it were a foreign language — any reader can easily see what kind of education I had. As it is written: "You can always tell a wise man by his speech, and his understanding and knowledge and teaching of the truth by what kind of language he uses."

But what good will it do to make excuses, even when I'm telling the truth? Especially since it seems foolish for an old man, like I am now, to yearn for the eloquence I missed out on when I was young. My sins came and snatched me away before I could finish my education. But who will believe me even if I say what I said before? I was just a boy, almost a child, when I was captured, before I knew what I should seek and what I should avoid. Even so, today I am very ashamed and afraid to show just how awkward my writing is. I am not able to explain things in just a few words like those who can write briefly. My mind and my spirit can't even work together so that my words say what I really feel inside.

If I had been given the same education as others, I could not keep silent because of my feelings of thankfulness to God. So perhaps it may seem to some people that I'm very presumptuous to write such a letter in my ignorant and sputtering style. Still, the Scripture does say: "A stammering tongue will quickly learn to speak peace." How much more ought I to make such an effort — I who am myself a letter of Christ for the work of salvation to the end of the earth. Even if I'm not written well, I'm still a solid and faithful letter, written in your hearts not with ink but with the spirit of the living God. As the Holy Spirit says: "Even unsophisticated people were created by God."

Once I was a crude and ignorant exile who didn't even know how I would take care of myself in the future. This much I know for certain — before God humbled me I was like a stone stuck deep in a mud puddle. But then God came along and with his power and compassion reached down and pulled me out, raised me up, and placed me on top of a wall. Because of this I must proclaim my good news, I must pay God back in some way for all that he has done for me here on earth and what he will do in eternity — blessings no one can even imagine.

So listen to me well, all of you, great and small, everyone who has any fear of God — especially you wealthy landowners so proud of your education — listen and consider this carefully: God chose foolish little me from among all of you who seem so wise and so expert in the law and so powerful in your eloquence. He picked ignorant Patrick ahead of all of you — even though I am not worthy — he picked me to go forth with fear and reverence — and without any of you complaining at the time — to serve the Irish faithfully. The love of Christ carried me here to be a help to these people for the rest of my life, if I may be worthy, and to work for them with humility and in sincerity.

Because of my faith in the Trinity, I must not worry about the consequences of this letter — I must choose to proclaim the gift of God and his everlasting help confidently and without fear, to make known his name everywhere, so that even after I die it might be a kind of spiritual legacy left behind for my brothers and sons, so many thousands I baptized for God.

I wasn't worthy nor was I really the sort of person for God to choose as his servant. God granted me this mission among the Irish after such hardship and so many troubles, after slavery, after many years — a future I certainly never hoped for or planned on when I was young.

After I came to Ireland I watched over sheep. Day by day I began to pray more frequently — and more and more my love of God and my faith in him and reverence for him began to increase. My spirit was growing, so that each day I would say a hundred prayers and almost as many each night, even during those times when I had to stay overnight in the woods or mountains. I would get up each morning before sunrise to pray, through snow and frost and rain. No harm came to me because of it, and I was certainly not lazy. I see now looking back that my spirit was bursting inside me.

One night while I was sleeping, I heard a voice saying to me: "You have fasted well — soon you will be going home." A short time after that I heard the voice again: "Behold, your ship is ready." The port wasn't nearby at all, maybe two hundred miles away, and I didn't know anyone who lived there. But I soon ran away and fled the master I had served for six years. I left trusting in God, who took care of me on my journey, and I wasn't afraid — at least until I came to the ship.

I arrived at the ship just as it was being launched and said that I would like to sail with them. The captain of the ship rejected the idea immediately and said angrily: "Forget about it — there's no way you're going with us!" When I heard this I started to walk away and go back to the hut where I had been staying. As I went along I began to pray. But before I had even finished my prayer, I heard one of the sailors coming up behind me and shouting: "Come back quickly, we want to talk with you." So I turned around and went back. The sailors then said to me: "Come on, we'll be glad to have you aboard — make a pact of friendship with us however you'd like." But I refused the pagan custom of sucking on their breasts because I feared God. Still, I hoped that they might eventually become Christians (they were all unbelievers). And so I climbed up on the ship, and immediately we set out to sea.

After three days we reached land, and for twenty-eight days after that we wandered through empty country. We didn't have any food, and hunger was making everyone weak. The next day the captain said to me: "Well, Christian, what are you going to do? You say this God of yours is so great and powerful — why don't you pray to him for us? We're dying of starvation here! I don't think we'll ever see another living soul again." But I answered him with great confidence: "Just turn with your whole heart to the Lord my God, because nothing is impossible for him. Today he's going to send food right into your path — plenty to fill your bellies — because his abundance is everywhere." And by the help of God that's exactly what happened. A large herd of pigs soon stumbled across the road in front of our very eyes. The sailors killed many of them and had a great pork feast for two nights — and their dogs also ate their fill (many of them had become very weak on the journey and were half dead). After this they offered great thanks to God, and they looked at me in a whole new way — with respect. From then on we had plenty of food. They even found some wild honey at one point and offered me a share. But then one of them said: "We've dedicated this as a sacrifice to the gods." Thank God I found out, because then of course I ate none of it.

That same night as I lay sleeping, I was attacked by Satan — an event I will remember for the rest of my days. He fell on me just like a huge rock so that I couldn't even move my arms or legs. Somehow it came to me at that moment, even in my ignorance, to call on the prophet Elijah for help. So as the sun began to rise, I shouted out with all my might: "Elijah! Elijah!" And as the rays of the sun touched my body, immediately all the weight and pain were lifted away. I believe that it was Christ the Lord who rescued me that night and that it was his spirit which cried out for my sake. Indeed, I hope that the same thing happens for me on the day of my judgment. For thus the gospel says: "On that day, the Lord says, it won't be you who is speaking, but the spirit of your Father will speak for you."

You know, there was another time many years later when I was also made a slave. On that first night when I was with my captors, then I heard a voice from Heaven saying to me: "You will be with them for only two months." And that's just what happened — after sixty days God liberated me from their hands.

Anyway, God provided for the sailors and myself on our journey. We had food and fire and good, dry weather for traveling every day, until we finally came to a settlement ten days later. As I said earlier, we had traveled through an empty land for twenty-eight days, and on the night we finally came across people we had run out of food again.

So after many years, I finally returned

home to my family in Britain. They took me in — their long-lost son — and begged me earnestly that after all I had been through I would never leave them again.

But one night while I was at home I saw a vision while sleeping — it was a man named Victoricus, coming to me as if he were arriving from Ireland. With him he brought a huge number of letters. He gave me one of them, and I saw that the first words were "The Voice of the Irish." When I began to read this letter, all of a sudden I heard the voices of those Irish who live near the woods of Foclut near the Western Sea. They called out to me with a single voice: "We beg you, holy boy, come here and walk among us!" I felt my heart breaking and was not able to read any more — and so I woke up. But thanks be to God, because after many years the Lord made their prayer come true.

There was another night when I heard the most beautiful words, a prayer — but I couldn't understand what was being said. Only God knows if the words were coming from inside me or were somewhere beyond me. But I did understand the very end of the prayer, which said: "The one who gave you your spirit, it is he who speaks in you." Then I woke up full of joy.

And there was another time I had a vision that I saw someone praying in me — it was as if I were actually inside my own body. I heard him above me — that is, in the internal me — and there he was praying forcefully with great sighs. While this was happening, I was stunned and baffled and kept asking myself, Who is this who is praying inside me? But at the end of the prayer he spoke to me and said he was the Spirit. Then I woke up and remembered what the apostle said: "The Spirit helps us when we don't know how to pray or what we ought to pray for. The Spirit prays with a language which goes beyond mere words." And again: "The Lord is our spokesman who prays for us."

When I was attacked by my superiors in the Church — those who accused me of sins contrary to my thankless role as a bishop — on that day I felt beaten down with such force that I thought I would never rise again, here in this life or in the next. But God spared me, a stranger and a foreigner, for the sake of his own name. With kindness and strength he rescued me from those who trampled on me. And I tell you, with those charges I was in some serious trouble! But I pray that God doesn't hold those accusations against them.

The pretense of their attack on me was that, after thirty years, they found out about a confession I had made in the days before I was even a deacon. At that time, because I was so troubled in my spirit, I let slip to my best friend something that I had done one day in my youth — not even a day but in an hour — because I was not yet then strong in my faith. I was, maybe, fifteen years old and didn't believe in the living God (I hadn't since my childhood). I remained in death and unbelief until God punished me severely and truly made me humble by hunger and nakedness day after day.

Believe me, I didn't go to Ireland willingly that first time — I almost died here. But it turned out to be good for me in the end, because God used the time to shape and mold me into something better. He made me into what I am now — someone very different from what I once was, someone who can care about others and work to help them. Before I was a slave, I didn't even care about myself.

When I was rejected by my superiors (as I mentioned earlier), I had another vision that very night — I saw my own face with shameful words of accusation written around it. But then I heard a divine voice saying to me: "We are very angry that my chosen one has been criticized." Notice that the voice said not, "*You* are angry" but "*We* are angry," as if God were speaking for both of us. For God says: "If someone harms you, it is as if he has poked me in the eye."

So I give thanks to the one who cared for me in all my difficulties, because he allowed me to continue in my chosen mission and the work that Christ my master taught me. More and more I have felt inside myself a great strength because my faith was proven right before both God and the whole world.

And so I boldly declare that my conscience does not trouble me now nor will it in the future — with God as my witness, I have not lied in the words I have written to you.

More than anything, I feel sorry for my best friend that we all had to hear what he said. I had entrusted to him the deepest secret of my heart. I even heard from some of my brothers that he had stood up for me back when they were deciding whether or not to make me a bishop (I wasn't in Britain at the time nor was it my idea). My friend was even the one who told me later: "You've made it! You're going to be a bishop!" — though I wasn't worthy of this. So why, out of the blue, did he later publicly disgrace me in front of everyone, good and bad alike? And over a matter that years earlier he had freely and gladly forgiven — as had God, who is greater than anyone.

Enough about this. But one thing I cannot be silent about is the gift of God that he gave to me here in this land of my slavery. I earnestly looked for him then and found him. He rescued me from all evil, I believe, because his spirit was alive in me and works through me even now. I know that is a bold thing to say, but God knows it's true. If some mere person had declared this to me, I would probably keep quiet about it because of Christ's love.

I must give thanks to my God continuously. He has helped me to keep my faith through difficult times, so that I can fearlessly offer myself as a kind of living sacrifice to Christ. The Lord has rescued me from so many dangers that sometimes I just have to ask: "God, who am I? What is it you want me to do?" You have worked beside me, helping me with your divine power, so that now I can praise and glorify your name constantly among nonbelievers — wherever I might be — in bad times and in good. Whatever happens to me, good or evil, I must accept it and give thanks to God. He has taught me to trust in him without any limits. God heard my prayers so that I, foolish though I am, might dare to undertake such a holy and wonderful mission in these last days — that I, in my own way, might be like those God said would come to preach and be witness to the good news to all nonbelievers before the end of the world. I have seen it happen — it has been done. I can testify that the good news has been preached to the very edge of the inhabited world.

It would take too long to tell you all about my work or even parts of it. But I will say that God in his great kindness often protected me from being enslaved, and he rescued me at least a dozen times from the threat of death. And the many other times I was in danger are just too numerous too mention — I don't want to bore my readers. God knows everything before it happens, so — with him as my witness — I can tell you he used to warn me frequently of trouble in advance, though I didn't deserve such special treatment.

From where did I get such wisdom? It certainly wasn't from inside myself. I didn't know my future, and I had no great knowledge of God. And later on, who was it who gave me such a wonderful and life-giving gift, the gift to know and love God? But to receive such things, I had to leave behind my home and family.

I have been offered many gifts here by those sorry for their sins — but I turned them all down. This angered some of my superiors, but with the help of God I fought back and did not give in to them (no thanks to my own will but by the power of God, who lives in me and resists them). I came to Ireland to preach the good news and to suffer abuse from unbelievers — and, it seems, to have my mission shamefully criticized. I have had many hard times, even to the point of being enslaved again, but I traded in my free birth for the good of others. If I am worthy, I am even ready to lay down my life willingly and without hesitation for his name. Here, in Ireland, is where I wish to live out my final days, if God will permit me.

I owe so much to God, who allowed so many people to find a new life in him through me. I confirmed them in our faith and ordained clergy for them everywhere, for a people just now coming to a belief in God. The master chose them from the ends of the earth, just as he said he would through the prophets: "The Gentiles will come to you from the ends of the earth and will say, 'Our ancestors worshiped false gods who cannot help us'." And Scripture also says: "I will place you like a lamp among the nonbelievers so that you may bring salvation to the ends of the earth."

And so I wish to remain here in Ireland and wait for the day he promised. For the gospel says: "They will come from the east and west, and from the north and south, to feast with Abraham, Isaac, and Jacob." As it says, so we believe — the faithful will come together from every part of the earth.

Because of this we ought to be very hardworking fishermen of souls. After all, the master urges us and teaches us when he says: "Follow after me and I will make you fish for people." The prophets also say: "Look, I send out many to fish and hunt, says God." And so on. It was necessary for me to spread out my nets so that I could bring in a big catch for God and so that there could be clergy to baptize and preach to these hungry, needy people.

Thus the Lord proclaims and urges and instructs us in the gospel, saying: "As you go, teach everyone and baptize them in the name of the Father, Son, and Holy Spirit — teaching them to do as I have told you. Behold, I will be with you even to the end of this age."

And again he says: "When you go into the whole world, preach the good news to every person. Whoever believes you and is baptized will be saved — whoever doesn't believe will be condemned."

He also says: "This good news of the kingdom will be declared in the whole world as a testimony to every land — and then the end will come."

The master also announces and declares through the prophet: "In the final days (he says) I will pour out my spirit on every person. Your sons will be prophets, your daughters and children will have visions, and your fathers will dream dreams. Indeed, into my servants, male and female, I will pour forth my spirit in those days and they will prophesy."

Finally, in the Book of Hosea, God says: "I will call those not my people 'my people' and will show mercy to those who have known no mercy. In the place where it was once said, 'You are not my people' — those will be called the children of the living God."

How wonderful it is that here in Ireland a people who never had any knowledge of God — who until now have worshiped idols and impure things — have recently become a people of the Lord and are now called children of God. You can see that the sons and daughters of Irish kings have become brothers and virgins for Christ.

One of these Irish women was of noble birth — full grown and quite beautiful really — whom I had baptized. A few days after this, she came to me with something important on her mind. She said that an angel from God had appeared to her and told her she should become a virgin of Christ if she wanted to be closer to God. Thanks be to God — six days later she joyfully and wholeheartedly chose that path which all virgins of God take.

But many of them do this against the wishes of their parents. Indeed, their families sometimes punish them cruelly and make all sorts of horrible accusations against them. Still, the number of such virgins who have chosen this new life continues to grow so that I can't keep track of them all. This doesn't even include widows and married women who abstain from sex. Sadly, of such women, the ones who suffer the most are the slaves. They face rape and constant threats but suffer this abuse bravely. God gives these women the grace to follow courageously in his path even though they are forbidden to do so.

Oh, how I would love to go home to Britain and see my family — and to Gaul to visit with the Christians there and see the holy people of God in person! But even if I wanted to leave behind these poor Irish women without any support, I am bound by the spirit of God, who would object and condemn me. I can't leave unfinished the work I've begun. Christ my master has commanded me to stay here in Ireland for the rest of my life — if God continues to want me here and if he will watch over me so that I follow his ways and keep away from any sinful action.

I certainly don't plan on sinning, but I don't trust myself as long as I am a mere human being. The tempter who every day tries to turn me from faith in God and the true religion is very strong — but I have dedicated myself to serve Christ my master to the bitter end. Human desires, however, are always dragging us toward death — to act out our sinful wishes. Heaven knows I have not led a perfect life (as some of you undoubtedly have), but I have made my peace with God and am not ashamed to stand before him. This I declare — from the time I was a young man, the love of God and respect for him has grown in me. Now I can say, as an old man, that with the help of God I have been faithful.

Laugh and make fun of me if you want to — I will not keep quiet, nor will I hide the signs and wonderful things that God revealed to me many years before they actually happened. For God knew everything that would occur even before the beginning of time.

I certainly do have to give thanks to God without ceasing, because he so often put up with my stupidity and carelessness. More than once he spared me from his much-deserved anger. He chose me to be his assistant, but I was slow to do as his spirit suggested. But my master had mercy on me so many times because he saw that I was ready — I just didn't know what to do under the circumstances.

Many people have tried to stop my mission in Ireland. I know they've talked to one another behind my back and said: "Why does this man want to work among these barbarians who don't know God?" I know they didn't say these things out of hatred but because it genuinely seemed foolish to them. I know — and they were right — that I seemed like an uneducated bumpkin. I didn't understand then as I do now the grace that God had granted to me.

So I have written this letter in my simple style to my brothers and fellow Christians. I hope you have believed me, because everything I have said and will keep on saying is to strengthen your faith. My wish is that you will do even better than I — for it always pleases a father to be surpassed by his children.

You know, as does God, how I have lived my life among you even when I was a young man — with a true faith and sincere heart. Also among the pagans of Ireland I have lived and will continue to live in honesty and truth. God knows I have cheated none of them — nor would I ever think of doing so — for the sake of God and his people. If I did wrong them, I might bring about the persecution of us all and they might curse the name of God. For it is written: "Woe to the person who causes God's name to be blasphemed."

Even though I'm not ignorant, I've tried very hard to preserve the integrity of myself, my Christian brothers, the virgins of Christ, and my faithful women followers. Some of this last group have been known to offer me small gifts and to place their jewelry on the altar as an offering, but I always returned it to them. They were shocked that I wouldn't accept these gifts, but I have to take the long-term view on this. I have to be very careful in these matters or some non-Christian might see it as an opportunity to criticize me and my ministry here. I cannot afford to give anyone even the smallest excuse to accuse me or defame my work.

I have baptized countless converts — did I ever ask any of them for even a small coin in return? Tell me and I will repay it. When God ordained so many clergy through my unworthy hands and I started them off in the ministry, did I ever ask even one of them to buy me a pair of shoes? Tell me and I'll give back the money.

In fact, it was just the opposite. I spent money to bribe the local kings to receive me. For your sake, my Irish Christians, I traveled everywhere among great dangers. I even went to the most remote parts of the island — places at the very edge of the world, places no one had ever been before — to baptize and ordain clergy and confirm people in the faith. I did it all, with the help of God, gladly and joyfully for your sake.

As I said, in my travels around the island, I used to make payments to the local kings. In addition, I also gave money to their sons who accompanied me on my journeys. But that didn't stop them from seizing me one time along with my companions. They were eager to kill me, but my time hadn't come yet — though they did steal everything we had and put me in chains. But after two weeks God in his power set me free and they returned all of our property. This was done by the grace of God and by the timely arrival of some old friends.

You all know very well how I paid out this money to those in power in those regions I have visited frequently. I've probably paid out enough to buy fifteen slaves, so that you could benefit from my teaching and so that I could enjoy being with you in God. I'm not sorry that I paid out bribes — in fact, I'm not finished yet. I spend money now and will spend even more. By the power of God, I may even spend my own life for your souls.

Please believe me — and I call on the power of God as my witness — I am not writing this letter looking for your admiration or money or even your thanks. I have enough honor of the quiet kind, hidden in my heart. God has promised me this, and he never lies.

It seems that I've become something of a celebrity in recent years, by God's will, even though I'm not the sort of person who should attract much attention. It's much better in this world to have poverty and troubles than riches and good times. After all, Christ our master became poor for all of us.

So I struggle on in my difficult life. Money? Even if I wanted to be rich, there's not much chance of that, believe me. On the contrary, every day I keep expecting to be murdered, assaulted, sold back into slavery, or some such thing. But I'm not afraid because I know Heaven waits for me. I throw myself on the mercy of God, who is in charge of everything. As the prophet says: "Turn your thoughts to God and he will take care of you."

So I will trust my spirit to my most faithful God. I serve here as his ambassador in spite of my shortcomings — but God doesn't use the world's standards in such matters. He chose me for this job — me, one of the least of his servants — to be his assistant.

I will try to pay God back for everything he has done for me. But how can I? What can I say or do for God? Everything I can do comes from him. But at least he can look inside me and judge my intent. He can see that I have been very willing to lay down my life in his service, as have others who loved him.

So may God never permit me to be separated from his people — for whom he worked so hard — here at the end of the earth. I pray that God will give me perseverance and allow me to be a faithful witness for him until I die.

If I have ever done anything worthwhile for the God I love, I ask that I might be allowed to die here for his name with these converts and slaves — even if it means that I won't have a marked grave or that my body is torn apart piece by piece by dogs or wild animals or that I serve as a meal for the birds of the air. I know if that were to happen, I would gain my soul along with a new body on that day we will undoubtedly rise again like the sun in the morning — like the son Jesus Christ our redeemer. We will become like children of the living God, brothers and sisters of Jesus, so that by him, through him, and in him, we will be like kings.

For the sun that we see with our eyes rises every day by the will of God, but it is not divine nor will its light remain. Everyone who worships that sun will face serious punishment someday, but we who believe in and follow Christ the true son will never really die. We will become forever as Christ has been always — ruling with God the all-powerful Father and the Holy Spirit now and forever — Amen.

I would write these words of my defense again and again if I could. I declare in truth and with joy in my heart — before God and his holy angels — that I have never had any motive in my work except preaching the good news and its promises. That is the only reason I returned here to

Ireland — a place I barely escaped from alive.

My final prayer is that all of you who believe in God and respect him — whoever you may be who read this letter that Patrick the unlearned sinner wrote from Ireland — that none of you will ever say that I in my ignorance did anything for God. You must understand — because it is the truth — that it was all the gift of God.

And this is my confession before I die.

Irish Names and Words

The pronunciation of Old Irish terms can be a challenge, even for native Irish speakers. Unlike in English and Modern Irish, there are no silent letters. Long vowels are marked with an accent, and words are normally stressed on the first syllable. The Irish *ch* is pronounced in the back of the throat, as in the German *ich* or the Scottish *loch*. Single consonants standing between vowels or at the ends of words are usually softened, as in the American English pronunciation of *later* as "lay-der." A *d* in this position is pronounced as the *th* in the English *bathe* and is shown here as *dh*.

Ailill	a-lil
Cathbad	kath-badh
Cú Chulainn	koo chulan
cumal	ku-wal
élúdach	ay-loo-dhach
Fáeth Fiada	fayth fia-dha
Fedelm	fedh-elm
Fergus mac Léti	fer-gus mak lay-di
Foclut	fok-lud

Ibar	i-var
imbas forosnai	im-bas for-os-na
Loíguire	loy-gu-ra
Medb	medh-av
Miliucc	mil-uk
Muirchú	mur-a-chu
Samain	sa-wan
Táin Bó Cuailnge	tan bow kual-nya
Tuatha Dé Danann	tua-tha day dan-an
Ulaid	u-ladh

Time Line

B.C.

753	Traditional date of the founding of Rome by Romulus and Remus
58–51	Julius Caesar conquers Gaul
55, 54	Julius Caesar attacks Britain, then withdraws
27	Roman Empire begins under Augustus Caesar

A.D.

c. 19	Strabo describes Ireland as a frozen land filled with cannibals
30	Jesus is executed by Roman authorities in Jerusalem
43	Roman conquest of Britain begins under Claudius
60	Druid stronghold on the Welsh island of Anglesey is destroyed by Romans
60–61	Revolt of Boudicca and the Iceni in Britain

64	Great fire in Rome; Nero persecutes Christians
78–84	Campaigns of Agricola in Britain
c. 98	Tacitus describes Ireland as well known to Roman merchants
112	Pliny writes to Emperor Trajan regarding Christians in Asia Minor
122	Construction begins on Hadrian's Wall across northern Britain
c. 150	Ptolemy publishes detailed map of Ireland
284	Diocletian becomes emperor
303	Persecution of Christians under Diocletian begins
306–337	Constantine the Great rules Roman Empire
356	Death of the monastic pioneer Anthony in Egypt
360s	Attacks by Picts, Saxons, and Irish on Britain
c. 372	Martin chosen as bishop of Tours in Gaul
379	Theodosius becomes Roman emperor
383	Magnus Maximus declared emperor of Britain

390s	Birth of Patrick (?)
406	Germanic invasions of Gaul begin
410	Alaric and Visigoths sack Rome; Roman rule in Britain ends
420	Jerome, translator of Latin Vulgate Bible, dies
429	Germanus travels to Britain to combat Pelagian heresy
430	Augustine of Hippo dies
431	Palladius arrives in Ireland as first bishop
c. 432	Ninian, missionary to Picts in southern Scotland, dies
445	Attila becomes sole ruler of the Huns
446	Britons appeal to the Roman general Aëtius for help
460s	Death of Patrick (?)
476	Romulus Augustulus, last Roman emperor in the West, is deposed
c. 521	The monastic founder Columba is born
c. 590	Columbanus leaves Ireland to found monasteries on the continent
600s	Muirchú and Tírechán compose lives of Patrick

c. 807   *Book of Armagh* is copied by Ferdomnach and assistants

Suggested Reading

There are so many good books available on ancient and early medieval times that a reader could spend the rest of his or her life happily learning more about the world of Rome, Celts, Christianity, Druids, Ireland, and Patrick. Listed here are what I consider some of the best and most helpful sources for each of the chapter topics.

1. The Early Years

Two biographies of Patrick that cover his life from childhood to old age are R. P. C. Hanson, *Saint Patrick: His Origins and Career* (1968) and E. A. Thompson, *Who Was Saint Patrick?* (1985). Each has its own point of view, but both are well worth exploring for anyone who wants to dig into the details and controversies of Patrick's life. The culture of Roman Britain in which Patrick grew up has attracted considerable attention in recent years. An excellent introduction to this distant province of the Empire is found in Barri Jones and David Mattingly, *An Atlas of Roman Britain* (1993), as well as S. Ireland,

Roman Britain: A Sourcebook (1986). If you want to know what it was like to be a Roman soldier stationed on Hadrian's Wall, I recommend Alan Bowman, *Life and Letters on the Roman Frontier* (1994).

2. Slavery

The cruelty and commerce of Roman slavery are discussed thoroughly in Keith Bradley, *Slavery and Society at Rome* (1994). The best introduction to Irish slavery and to early Irish culture in general is Fergus Kelly, *A Guide to Early Irish Law* (1988). I have benefited immensely from this fascinating book and Kelly's subsequent *Early Irish Farming* (2000). For the long history of contact between the Mediterranean world and Ireland, I would modestly recommend my own *Ireland and the Classical World* (2001).

3. Escape

To understand the physical landscape and challenges of Patrick's journey through the bogs and mountains of Ireland, there is no better guide than the *Atlas of the Irish Rural Landscape* (1997), edited by F. H. A. Aalen, Kevin Whelan, and Matthew Stout. This beautifully illustrated work covers Irish geography, climate, and settlement patterns from the last Ice Age to the present day.

4. Home

The "Fall of Rome" has always been something of a misnomer, but the transition between Roman rule and what came afterward in Patrick's Britain and elsewhere in western Europe is aptly covered in the many readable works of the historian Peter Brown. An excellent starting point is his *World of Late Antiquity* (1989). For Britain in particular, Michael Jones, *The End of Roman Britain* (1996), surveys the decline of Roman power on the island. For those desiring a comprehensive look at these formative times, the essays and articles in *Late Antiquity: A Guide to the Postclassical World* (2000), edited by G. W. Bowersock, Peter Brown, and Oleg Grabar, can provide many hours of worthwhile browsing.

5. The Missing Years

There are enough books available on early Christianity to fill anyone's library, but I recommend going back to the original sources as much as possible. The New Testament, of course, is an easy read in many modern translations, but the documents left behind by Romans, church councils, and early Christian writers provide a fascinating picture of the spread of a new religion. These can be found in many works, including *Documents of the Christian Church* (1967), edited by Henry Bettenson. Augustine's *Confessions*, available in a number of good translations, tells a story very different from, but no less interesting than, that in Patrick's letters. You can judge for yourself if Pelagius was a heretic by reading his work in *Pelagius: Life and Letters* (1998), edited by B. R. Rees. Henry Chadwick, *The Early Church* (1967), is still an excellent survey of the entire subject of early Christianity, while Charles Thomas, *Christianity in Roman Britain to A.D. 500* (1981), is a useful secondary source on the Church in Roman Britain.

6. Return to Ireland

Saint Patrick's World (1993) by Liam de Paor provides far and away the best introduction to the religious setting of Ireland and the bringing of Christianity to the island. This wonderfully readable collection of essays and original documents in translation should be the starting point for anyone interested in early Irish Christianity. Two important secondary sources on the period are Dáibhí Ó Cróinín, *Early Medieval Ireland, 400–1200* (1995), and T. M. Charles-Edwards, *Early Christian Ireland* (2000). The culture that Patrick encountered in Ireland is also illuminated by Barry Raftery's *Pagan Celtic Ireland* (1994).

7. Kings

The story of kingship in early Ireland is best told in Francis John Byrne, *Irish Kings and High-Kings* (1987), and Nerys Patterson, *Cattle-lords and Clansmen: The Social Structure of Early Ireland* (1994). David McCullough gives a sweeping history of the topic in *Wars of the Irish Kings* (2002). The kingship initiation and other raucous tales of bestiality and piety can be read in Gerald of Wales, *History and Topography of Ireland*, translated by John J. O'Meara (1982).

8. Druids

The topic of Celtic religion, and the Druids in particular, has produced an incredible number of books, many of which should be approached with great caution. I recommend Proinsias Mac Cana, *Celtic Mythology* (1983), and Miranda Green, *Celtic Myths* (1993), as solid introductions. The Druids in ancient times are reliably presented in Stuart Piggott, *The Druids* (1975), and Miranda Green, *The World of the Druids* (1997).

There are many excellent guides to the

world of the ancient Celts, with Barry Cunliffe, *The Ancient Celts* (1997), being one of the best. John Haywood, *Atlas of the Celtic World* (2001), is a superb visual guide to Celtic culture, as H. D. Rankin, *Celts and the Classical World* (1987), is a clear introduction to the classical sources. These ancient sources are collected and translated in my *War, Women, and Druids* (2002). The artistic tradition is beautifully surveyed in Ruth and Vincent Megaw, *Celtic Art* (1989). Early Irish stories are collected and translated in Jeffrey Ganz, *Early Irish Myths and Sagas* (1981), Thomas Kinsella, *The Táin* (1969), and Patrick Ford, *The Celtic Poets* (1999), along with John Koch and John Carey, *The Celtic Heroic Age* (2000).

9. Virgins

The life of women in the ancient Mediterranean world is illustrated, sometimes surprisingly, by the original sources in *Women's Life in Greece and Rome* (1992), edited by Mary R. Lefkowitz and Maureen B. Fant. For early Ireland, see Christina Harrington, *Women in a Celtic Church: Ireland 450–1150* (2002). Female mythological figures such as Medb and Epona are discussed in Miranda Green, *Celtic Goddesses* (1995).

10. The Ends of the Earth

James Romm surveys Greek and Roman views of the boundaries of the world in *The Edges of the Earth in Ancient Thought* (1992). The daring voyage of the fourth-century B.C. explorer Pytheas to the northern seas of Europe is discussed by Barry Cunliffe in *The Extraordinary Voyage of Pytheas the Greek* (2002). Bernard McGinn covers the lively history of apocalyptic thought in Christianity in *Visions of the End* (1998).

11. Coroticus

Christopher Snyder gives readers a glimpse into the time of tyrants in Britain after the end of Roman power in *The World of King Arthur* (2000). For the best early source on these rulers of post-Roman Britain, read the scathing critique of the sixth-century churchman Gildas in his *Ruin of Britain* (1978), edited and translated by Michael Winterbottom.

12. Confession

There have been several good editions of Patrick's *Confession* in English, but I recommend Thomas O'Loughlin, *Saint Patrick: The Man and His Works* (1999), for further study of this amazing letter. He provides an excellent translation with insightful introductions and an exhaustive index to Patrick's biblical references, along with a copious bibliography of recent Patrician studies. The older translation and notes of Ludwig Bieler in *The Works of St. Patrick* (1953) are still valuable as well.

13. Ireland After Patrick

Many of the original stories and writings of the early Irish saints are found in Oliver Davies, *Celtic Spirituality* (1999), as well as Adomnán's own *Life of St. Columba*, translated by Richard Sharpe (1995). John J. O'Meara presents the *Voyage of Saint Brendan* in a faithful translation with a helpful introduction (1991). I would also recommend Thomas O'Loughlin's sober reading of Celtic Christianity in *Celtic Theology* (2000) and Máire Herbert's excellent *Iona, Kells, and Derry* (1996). The original Old Irish *Breastplate* poem is found in Whitley Stokes and John Strachan, *Thesaurus Paleohibernicus*, vol. 2, 354–58 (1903).

Epilogue: Patrick's Letters

The most complete Latin edition of Patrick's letters is Ludwig Bieler, *Libri Epistolarum Sancti Patricii Episcopi* (reprint, 1993). An alternative view of Patrick's Latin text is presented in the edition of D. R. Howlett, *The Book of Letters of Saint Patrick the Bishop* (1994).

About the Author

Philip Freeman is a professor of Classics at Washington University in St. Louis. He earned his Ph.D. in Classical Philology and Celtic Studies from Harvard University. The author of three previous books, he lives with his family in Clayton, Missouri.

The employees of Thorndike Press hope you have enjoyed this Large Print book. All our Thorndike and Wheeler Large Print titles are designed for easy reading, and all our books are made to last. Other Thorndike Press Large Print books are available at your library, through selected bookstores, or directly from us.

For information about titles, please call:

(800) 223-1244

or visit our Web site at:

www.gale.com/thorndike
www.gale.com/wheeler

To share your comments, please write:

Publisher
Thorndike Press
295 Kennedy Memorial Drive
Waterville, ME 04901